PRAISE for A SEA

"Dr. Williamson has motivated, inspired and educated thousands of people about the reality of human trafficking in our country. For many years, she has known that when one generation accepts the myths of prostitution, the next will embrace it. She is passionate about breaking these myths and embracing long-term, permanent, systemic change. I consider her my mentor and hero."

-Theresa Flores

Theresa Flores is a survivor of and campaigner against sex trafficking, and the creator of Save Our Adolescents from Prostitution, a nonprofit organization that aims to help prevent sex trafficking.

"Dr. Celia Williamson is an indispensable leader in our fight against human trafficking in her home of Toledo and around the country. Her passion has opened so many eyes to the ways people are bought and sold in our own backyards, and uplifted survivors' voices. Dr. Williamson's innovative work has influenced policymakers throughout the U.S. and around the world, and has helped us make real progress in this fight."

-Senator Sherrod Brown
Senior United States Senator from Ohio

"Dr. Williamson is an important human rights leader for the state of Ohio. She is a key leader in pushing to end human trafficking in our lifetime."

-Senator Teresa Fedor
Senior United States Senator from Ohio

"Celia Williamson is an inspirational leader, a scholar of unequivocal integrity, and an activist whose vision for social justice is rivaled only by her sheer determination to see that vision achieved. In compelling fashion, this memoir pays tribute to the groundbreaking work that defines Dr. Williamson (i.e., creating the first direct service anti-trafficking program in Ohio, building the first local anti-trafficking coalition, and developing the oldest human trafficking and social justice conference in the nation), and provides insight into critical developmental experiences that set her life's work into motion. Dr. Williamson is a true change-maker who, in this personal account, invites each of us to journey with her and rise to the challenge."

-Rochelle Dalla, PhD
Editor-in-Chief, *Journal of Human Trafficking*

"Dr. Celia Williamson is a leader in the anti-sex trafficking research field and has been critically important in the development of knowledge to support victims. Dr. Williamson's early work on the streets working with prostituted women led us to see through our biases and pre-conceptions to find violence, coercion, and a person worth dignity and respect. This book captures the spirit of Dr. Williamson and should motivate each of us to not just to do more,
but something real for social justice."

-Dominique Roe-Sepowitz, PhD
Director of the Arizona State University
Office of Sex Trafficking Intervention Research

A SEAT AT THE TABLE

The Courage to Care About Trafficking Victims

Celia Williamson, PhD

Distinguished Professor

Director, MSW Program

Executive Director, Human Trafficking and Social Justice Institute

School of Social Justice

A Seat at the Table: The Courage to Care About Trafficking Victims

ISBN-13: 978-0-578-55969-8

Printed in the United States of America

A Seat at the Table

The Courage to Care About Trafficking Victims

"Dr. Williamson is a true change-maker who, in this personal account, invites each of us to journey with her and rise to the challenge."

-Rochelle Dalla, PhD., Editor in Chief, Journal of Human Trafficking

Celia Williamson, PhD

To all of the survivors who have the courage to still care and fight for their freedom, and to the advocates for putting their courage into action.

To my daughter, Lisa, for being the most precious jewel in the family crown, and to my life partner, Jeff, for making sure I'm wearing my crown and that the jewel in it shines.

Also, thank you to Tom and Judy Gutteridge, for putting their belief in the freedom of others into action.

CONTENTS

a MODERN DAY SLAVERY

Under the law, sex trafficking is identified as recruiting, harboring, transporting, providing, or obtaining someone for the purposes of a commercial sex act through the use of force, fraud, or coercion, or if that person is under the age of eighteen. The International Labor Organization conservatively estimates that there are 12.3 million human trafficking victims in the world today, while research from other non-governmental organizations puts the number at 27 million. The U.S. government calls these victims "modern day slaves," and these slaves are victims of sex and/or labor trafficking who work for the financial profit of someone else. Victims are often threatened and afraid to tell authorities. They suffer repeated rapes, physical abuse, and psychological torture at the hands of their traffickers as well as their customers.

Society often blames sex trafficking victims for their own victimization, branding them as "whores" and prosecuting them as "prostitutes." We've been taught to look down our noses at women involved in the sex trade under the assumption that they've chosen to trade sex for money. We associate sex work with poor character, a lack of morality, and low intelligence. And it starts when we're young, as the patriarchy infiltrates our perspective with gendered biases about women's bodies. We call girls who dress outside of society's expectations "sluts." We crack jokes and call our girlfriends "prostitutes" and "whores" for sleeping around. We laugh at our own internalization of sexism without ever thinking about what role sex trafficking plays in the world of street prostitution. For many people, privilege affords them that ignorance.

I wasn't afforded that privilege. Being born and raised at ground zero—a black girl in a poor urban neighborhood in Toledo, Ohio—I grew up on the same block where prostitutes worked, where women were kidnapped and raped, where we were groomed for the undergound economy, having been shut out from and ignored by white America. This is the true story of four girls living in a poor neighborhood in Ohio in the seventies, and how their cultural exposure to sex trafficking left one of them dead, two of them entangled in the seemingly inescapable world of trafficking, and me, a survivor, who went on to obtain my PhD and become an internationally recognized expert on the topic.

This book exposes the barriers and challenges I faced—culturally, racially, and socioeconomically—as well as my successes and accomplishments. It is an education of the street, of poor black and marginalized culture, of the oppression that modern communities of color endure, and of the insidious dangers that lurk where no one is looking.

This book is also for social workers, those in the field, students, and educators. As an authentic advocate, and as one of the first in the field to conduct actual street outreach with trafficked women and youth—from going into crack houses to working with women, engaging pimps and drug dealers, running support groups and therapeutic groups with women, and interviewing trafficked youth, to working collaboratively with politicians to pass three state laws and one federal law, to building a thriving community-wide coalition, a state commission on trafficking, an internationally successful conference on the topic, and a global organization of human trafficking scholars—it is my intention with this book to pass on my knowledge and my expertise so that research can continue and programs can flourish. In this book, I detail the struggles I overcame and the successes I achieved, providing readers with ways they can get involved in their communities to make freedom a reality for everyone. More specifically, each chapter builds on the next, moving from my personal story involving trafficked friends, to engaging on both micro level one-on-one work with victims to macro level organizational and policy work.

I was nearly destined to be a trafficking victim. I was born with all of the right risk factors and immersed in circumstances that offered me few other choices. I had to work twice as hard for just as much as someone from the middle class, and it wasn't easy. But I went from stereotypical to atypical, granting me with the unique insight, skillset, and a degree of empathy that has allowed me to connect academic concepts with action, policy to people, and experience with education. It takes courage to do this work, but there is nothing more rewarding in the world than spreading freedom. **And when we find the courage to care, we find the courage to create change.**

the **ANTI-TRAFFICKING MANIFESTO**

Slavery around the world today is as real as it was hundreds and thousands of years ago. Human trafficking is modern day slavery. It manifests in the taking of someone's freedom so that someone else can profit. I want to remind you that there is not a freedom you enjoy today that was not bought and paid for by the struggle and the pain and the marching and the picketing and the bleeding and the dying and the silent suffering of others.

Thank God for the advocates, the agitators, the rebellious, the dissenters, the protesters, and the disputers.

It was because these "trouble makers" cared about humanity, cared that freedom be a reality for those in the world that have it. Because, most often, it was not the people in the White House or state houses that brought about the social change needed to fight for human rights; it was always the people outside the buildings, yelling and demanding, not willing to spend one more day without the humane treatment of others and themselves, that always made the difference. These advocates cared. Fighting trafficking means we care about the freedom of others. When we have the courage to care, and put our caring into organized action, amazing things can happen.

WHEN WE CARE,

we can work to make sure a rescued child can fall asleep every night without fear of being raped again and forced to work.

We can work to make sure a foreign survivor feels at home in our country and in the world. And we can make sure laws are passed that not only help one, but help the many.

WHEN WE CARE,

we can work to help a survivor find the courage to finally testify against her trafficker.

We can work to make sure a twelve-year-old knows that he is loved and wanted, regardless of how hard he had to work for little or no pay in the past, or what he has to give you now.

And we can help a woman who was sold to the highest bidder talk about it for the first time.

WHEN WE CARE,

we can make sure a teen respects and appreciates her body, and dreams of what her mind can do.

We can make sure a traumatized and trafficked woman sees past her demons.

And we can help a man that was beaten and forced to work feel like a man again.

WHEN WE CARE,

we can make policy-makers change laws, educate the community so they know what to look for, how to identify victims, and require systems to respond effectively.

WHEN WE CARE,
we can make sure a drug-addicted survivor
puts down the needle and deals with her past.

We can make a faith-based community use their
time to put their love and faith into practice.

And we can make a family forever grateful
for the return of their recovered daughter.

WHEN WE CARE,
we can make forgotten people who live in the shadows
be recognized, receive justice, and reintegrate
them back into their communities.

And we can help a survivor who has been
rescued celebrate a lifetime of freedom.

And we can do this every day.

Because Martin Luther King, Jr. cared, we have civil rights for all people. Because Caesar Chavez cared, we work to improve the treatment of migrant workers. Because Harvey Milk, Susan B. Anthony, Rosa Parks, Gloria Steinem, Audre Lorde, and Ghandi cared...

Because you care, that's what brought you to this book.

Those who have the courage to care transform
everything that they touch, and nothing on earth
is higher than that, nothing more sacred,

for it takes great courage to care.

PART I

I heard a story that if you put a frog in a hot pot of boiling water that it will quickly jump out, but if you put the frog in cold water and slowly heat the water up to a boil, the frog will stay in the water until it cooks to death.

CHAPTER ONE
China Doll

I heard the buzzing of my mother's alarm clock and rolled over in the morning twilight. Her feet hit the living room floor, and I tracked her movement as I heard her take hurried steps through the dining room and into the bathroom. After quickly readying herself, I listened for the click of the stove, the skillet to hit the burner, and the beginning sizzle of bacon. That meant my mother would soon be running into my room to yell at me to get up.

I waited with the sheets half torn down already, but my mother didn't throw my door open like she normally did. I lifted my head to listen for her, and I could hear her frantically shuffling from room to room, opening drawers and cabinets and then slamming them shut, muttering to herself. Her muttering escalated to shouting, and, before long, my mother swung my door open in mid-sentence.

"Where are my earrings?" she frantically shouted at me.

I blinked at her, adjusting to the morning, "I don't know."

My mother grit her teeth while staring at me, her hand still clenching the doorknob.

"You better tell me where my earrings are, Celia," my mother sharply demanded.

I looked over at my sister, Camille, still lying in her bed. She shook her head to say she didn't know either. Frustration took me over, and I pulled myself up out of my bed, looking directly at my mother, her face still fuming.

"I don't know, Ma. I didn't lose them, so good luck finding them," I told her, looking away to pick up my socks.

Before I could reach my socks, my mother had run up to me and smacked me across the face. This sting of her hand burned my cheek, and I looked down and away from her. I was in shock. My mother had never hit me before. The wild look in her eyes was something I'd noticed brewing for a while, but I never expected her to snap on me. The room fell silent for a moment as she pointed at me and then to my sister.

"You better find those earrings, and watch your mouth," she warned, and then stormed out of the room, leaving the door ajar behind her.

Camille shook her head, rolled out of bed, and started to collect her things for the day. I did the same. There was nothing to say. After slipping on my socks, I washed my face off and headed to the kitchen.

As quickly as my mother had gotten fired up, so did she cool. While smoking a cigarette and sipping on her first cup of coffee, she handed me my breakfast plate. I looked into her face for a moment, searching, and found what I was looking for—that smile behind her eyes.

The one that told me she hadn't meant to hit me, that told me I shouldn't worry about it happening again. I took my plate to the table as my grandmother came in through the kitchen door.

Everyone in the neighborhood entered and exited my mother's kitchen throughout the day. Coffee and conversation was always on from breakfast till dinner. Cigarette smoke filled the room, my mother was always greasing a pan for the next meal, and her and her friends spent the day laughing, arguing, and running the numbers at our kitchen table. Everyone loved my mother's cooking and loved to gossip with her. Her kitchen table was the center of the neighborhood, central to the universe in my young mind. Everything that happened in the neighborhood was discussed at my mother's kitchen table. Issues were debated, gossip flew, and both covert and overt plans were devised. Who did what, who said what, and what neighbors at the table would do about what was happening was being served each day, including who borrowed money, who broke up, who was angry, and who was plotting against whom. When adults came in, the kids were asked to get up and give their seats. You had to earn your right to sit at the table and to join the conversation.

I sat by the big box furnace while my mother left the kitchen oven on and open for heat. There was a racket at the front door when the milkman left our delivery on the porch. I went running to the porch as soon as I heard the glass bottles hit the pavement. Grabbing one large bottle at a time, I used both of my arms and part of my chest and stomach to try and balance the weight, and I carried the bottles from the porch to the refrigerator. The weight of the bottles made me feel like I was powerful, and it gave me a sense of pride to help my mother. I wouldn't let anyone help me. I'd deemed this chore to be mine alone.

As I walked in and out of the kitchen, my mother and grandmother never looked up from the table. They were used to me grabbing the milk, and they were busy playing the numbers. They sat together, studying the numbers, even looking through dream books and numerology texts that were so old they were barely still bound. They used dingy sheets of paper with lines of numbers and dates when, as they said, "the number fell," meaning it was the day the winning number would be announced.

"I'm figuring the number!" my mother snapped at my grandmother, who was trying to show her a forecast she'd contrived from one of her books. With the same seriousness of an important business meeting on Wall Street, my mother and grandmother diligently studied which numbers they would play for the day.

"Hand me that paper there, Celia," without looking up, my mother stretched out her arm for me to hand her the Sunday paper.

Opening the newspaper, she always turned to the stocks and bonds. Before the lottery was legal, poor people played in the illegal numbers game, and you could choose to play the stocks or the bonds. Everyone knew which numbers were the previous day's winners by looking in the business section of the paper. Playing a dime or a quarter was too expensive for my family's budget. My mother and grandmother typically played a nickel each, with the chance to win five to twenty-five dollars, depending on whether they boxed it—meaning the three numbers they chose could fall in any combination—or if they played it straight—meaning the numbers had to fall exactly the way the player predicted it. Playing it straight always paid more.

"But look here, Charlotte," my grandmother implored my mother, strongly pointing to a different page in her book.

My mother brushed her off and left the table, shooing me out of her way as she exited the kitchen. I finished putting the last milk bottle into the refrigerator as my mother went to meet the numbers man at the door to give him her bet.

My grandmother sat in silence. I stared. We never really interacted, and at five years old, I still hadn't started talking to anyone yet. It was understood that my grandmother didn't really have an interest in me or my sisters, and the feeling was mutual.

I watched from around the corner as my mother handed the numbers man her money, and I noticed him look at her with affection. Everyone loved my mother. She always wore bright colors and ruffled shirts, especially in red and orange. Her jet-black hair was always coifed on top of her head in big, bold curls that rolled from the front to the back, with bangs that hung down just above her eyes. She was cool and casual in the way she dragged on cigarettes. She was beautiful, and she always had a cup of coffee by her side. She was a gregarious woman who talked all of the time. She could crack jokes with anyone, and she had a hardy, confident laugh that filled the room. Like any good housewife, my mother loved to gossip about everything and everyone in the neighborhood. Occasionally, she argued with the neighbors, but mostly talked behind their backs.

Conversely, when my mother was upset, everyone knew it. When something threw her into an anxious panic, my mother would scream all through the house at the top of her lungs, and all of the neighbors knew to keep their distance. In the same way that my mother was the most endearing and interesting person to be around, she could also be the scariest. There was no middleground with her, and her extreme personality was taxing on those of us that had to live with her. There was never an opportunity to take time away from it, but the neighbors were able to carefully measure their distance from her. They wanted to be around my mother, but only when she was in good spirits.

Our neighborhood was full of dynamic personalities, so my mother's extremism fit in well there. Being a small town in urban Ohio made up of very low-income families, there were a lot of children in the neighborhood from all different cultural striations. A Mexican family with six kids lived next door to us, and there were a few white Appalachian families that had migrated from West Virginia, Alabama, and Tennessee with at least five kids in each family, including Emma Kay Dolberry's family. My parents had five girls of their own, and everyone in our neighborhood counted on one another. We borrowed food and money from one another and made sure that everyone was equally cared for the best we could. We had to be an insular support system for each other to keep afloat because it was hard to survive outside of our community, and no one ever left.

Emma Kay Dolberry lived three doors down from me. She was white, from an Appalachian family, had seven siblings, and no toys. Her family had very little. Emma's father had migrated to Adrian, Michigan from Alabama, and her mother had come from Tennessee. They met after both moved to Toledo in search of work. Life was tough for the Dolberrys, but they were hard-working people if nothing else. Emma's family lived in a one-story, two-bedroom house like ours, but she often came and stayed at my house for a week at a time. Since it was just me and Camille now, we had more room for Emma in our bedroom than she had in her own home.

Emma was a tiny girl with short, sandy colored hair, cut in a bowl style. She had a mother and father that lived together, but they drank and fought a lot, which also encouraged Emma Kay to stay with us often. While our house was mostly quiet and tense with apprehension, Emma Kay's house was loud and explosive.

Emma and I loved to play with Barbies. We'd cut shoeboxes in half and pull cloth over them to make couches for our dolls. We stuck different colored sewing pins in the earlobes of our Barbies for earrings, and we cut out small pictures in magazines to create props inside the intricate dioramas we built. We'd dress them up and imagine different social situations and have conversations with them all day. We used Ken dolls and GI Joe as their boyfriends, but we both preferred GI Joe over Ken, because, unlike Ken, he could stretch his arm around Barbie. The Ken doll's arm just jutted out like a board if you lifted it. You could find me and Emma Kay tucked away in my bedroom most days, with Barbies and Barbie apartments sprawled across my bedroom floor.

We built tents, ate sandwiches and pizza at my house, walked to school and back home together, and told all of our secrets to each other. We looked alike. We were the same height, same weight, and both had short brown hair and brown eyes. We called each other sister and told everyone we were twins, though she was white and I was black. When we rode our bikes together, we called ourselves the Black and White Taxi Cab Company, reveling not in our differences but in our friendship. I loved Emma Kay, and she was my one true connection to belonging as a child.

Our lives occurred within a four-block radius. Major streets outlined the boundaries of our neighborhood within which we felt safe and were with each other. Cherry Street and Lagrange, Bancroft Street and Oneida served as the main outlines for our neighborhood in each direction—the barriers that contained our community. While we ventured into other neighborhoods once in a while, it was always for a specific purpose, but we never crossed to the other side of Cherry Street. The kids there were not a part of who we were. We went to the store and home. No one went to the mall or on vacation. Everything that happened, happened in our neighborhood, and my family only interacted with two systems outside of our streets when they had to: the healthcare system and the school system.

While Lagrange Street was notorious for prostitution, I never knew it. It was also a family street with a few locally owned bars on it, houses that people in the neighborhood rented, a gas station, a library, and a few social service agencies for the poor. Lagrange Street was simply part of my neighborhood—an asphalt line within which my family lived and functioned; a boundary of my community. I didn't know anything else, and as a young girl, I didn't have the capacity to imagine the likes of prostitution or real crime yet. I was blind to it then.

My family was the most financially stable in the neighborhood, but while my father put on a shirt and tie for work every day, he was turned down for a loan to buy land so he could build us a house in a better neighborhood. Racism and discrimination ruled the way we had to live, because while the white families in our neighborhood were bound there by poverty, we were tethered to the neighborhood by segregation. We were simply blocked from living a better life. It didn't matter if my parents had enough money to get us out, because society didn't have anywhere for us to go.

When my father was born, his parents weren't issued a birth certificate—another black baby was born and no one cared. As a young kid, he made ten cents a day helping an older gentleman peddle fruit and vegetables up and down the neighborhoods. At seventeen, my father entered the Navy by lying about his age. Since he didn't have a birth certificate, he simply went to the Health Department office, told them it was his eighteenth birthday, and they printed and issued him a birth certificate to produce for the Navy recruiter.

My parents married in 1944 to the disappointment of my mother's parents. My mother was a very light-skinned Episcopalian woman of mixed raced—her mother was white and her father was an educated light-skinned African-American—and her parents didn't want her marrying a dark-skinned Baptist. There was a common joke among black people then: "What do you call a black man that can read? An Episcopalian." To them, he wasn't deserving of my mother, and he didn't pass the "brown paper bag test," meaning he was darker than a brown paper bag, making him unworthy of my mother, but my mother didn't listen. She knew what she wanted and married him anyway.

Shortly after the wedding, my father bought our house for

$4,000. It was a two-bedroom home, and I was the youngest of five, so I slept in the same room with all four of my sisters before three of them moved out. By the time I came along, the house was replete with sixties-era furnishings: blonde end tables and comfortable, though worn out, furniture.

My father was a short, dark-skinned man with a booming voice and an intimidating presence. He was always gone. In his life before me, my father had seen a short stint of fame as a the first African-American man to win a gold medal for officiating boxing matches in the Olympics. My father approached life like he approached boxing: go for it with all that you have and win. Once an award-winning boxer himself, he put all that he had into being successful in business and being recognized as such. My father joined the Masons and spent most evenings at the lodge with his friends. When he wasn't there, he was at the Baptist church across town, building political connections. But as hard as my father pulled on his bootstraps to lift his family and himself to a new level, he was continually beaten down and blocked by racist practices. Though he never quit, gifting me with that same tenacity, I suspect my father had been beaten down by the loss of his dreams by the time his children were born. Now, he was a stark man with an ominous presence who the neighbors feared. He rarely spoke to any of us, and his intimidating nature kept him on the fringe of our family, coming and going as he pleased without really participating in our household.

Dad put on a suit and tie every day to go to work at the government's automotive tank division in Warren, Michigan. He spent two hours just on his commute each day, but he never missed a day of work.

He made that commute in snowstorms, torrential downpours, and during tornado warnings for almost forty years. My father wanted to work, and he was ambitious, but the fruits of his labor were always denied. He would tell stories about asking for raises and never getting more than three cents at a time—his white bosses always commenting, "How would that look if we gave you a noticeable raise?"

Over the years, though, his salary quietly crept up, until he was finally able to ask the bank for a loan of $500 to buy property in a rural area that now boasts half-million-dollar homes, but he was turned down. The only place where he was qualified to buy a home was a few blocks from the strip of bars reserved for blacks, a couple of blocks away from downtown Toledo. Redlined, we lived in our north end neighborhood, marginalized and oppressed by a society that didn't value our lineage, my father's contributions, or his hard work. My father was, however, accepted in the boxing world, and so he traveled a lot, helping to train boxers and referee bouts for the Golden Gloves and amateur boxing. Between his job, lodge meetings, working on houses, boxing and travel, my father had a full life, but not with us.

Over the years, unable to move us out of our neighborhood, my father collected houses on our block. He first purchased a building with three apartments that sat across the street from our house. Later, he would come to own much more of the neighborhood, including both houses on either side of ours plus six others on the block. By the end of the nineties, there was only one house on the block that my father didn't own, which he soon purchased, but his rise in real estate meant that he was never home while I was growing up. When he wasn't working at the plant or at a "meeting," he was flipping the dilapidated properties in our neighborhood, collecting rents from people who could barely afford it, rarely collecting a deposit.

Outside of work and his hobbies, my father disappeared into the homes of women I didn't know. He provided for our family—unlike our neighbors, we always had enough food, clothes on our backs, and the utilities never shut off—but he did no more for us than that. Like my grandmother, my father wasn't interested in a relationship with us—no one seemed to be besides my mother, and that relationship was tenuous and fraught with problems.

By lunchtime, our kitchen was full of smoke and women. I could hear them gossiping and laughing from my room, and I avoided going into the kitchen unless I had to. There wasn't much for me to do after my sisters headed to school, and Emma Kay hadn't come around yet, so I spent much of the morning playing on the couch, wrapped in the blankets my mother slept in, until she called me for lunch. I rolled off of the couch and silently headed for the kitchen.

I entered the hazy room. The linoleum tile felt warm against my feet from all of the foot traffic coupled with heat buzzing from the stove. My mother handed me a small plate with bacon, eggs, and toast on it, and before I could turn around to leave with it, she caught my shoulder.

"Miss Amelia said something funny today," Mother said to me while pointing across the table at her friend. "We were talkin' about you all, and Miss Amelia says you look like a little China doll. Those eyes and that skin. Yep, I think she got it right." With that, my mother turned and sat back down, picking up her cigarette from the ashtray.

I left the kitchen, set my plate aside, and slipped into the bathroom to study my face. I had to think about what my mother said to me. *Those eyes and that skin.* My eyes were a little slanted, and my skin tone was light, like smooth brown porcelain. I was very short and small with a thin frame and a round face that made my head look bigger than my body. As I looked over myself, I felt pride in what my mother said. She had complimented me, and compliments were hard to come by in our house.

Confident, I came swinging out of the bathroom and back into the kitchen with a smile on my face. I wanted to revel in my mother's compliment a little longer and show myself off. My mother and her friends looked over at me and started to laugh.

"She sure does look like a China doll," Miss Amelia confirmed, and I smiled at her with gratitude.

My mother laughed while looking at me, adding, "That's because China dolls are empty-headed mannequins like you."

"What's a mannequin?" I asked.

"It's a dummy," Mom snapped quickly.

In an instant, I fell from elated to crushed. I watched my mother's lips curl into a laugh through the smoky kitchen, and I felt small and far away from her in that moment. The floor fell out from beneath me, and I inched my way out of the kitchen, backing into the living room and out of sight.

My heart beat hard against my chest, and the air around me grew thin. It was harder and harder to breathe by the moment, and I rushed into the bathroom to hide. My face was red, and my eyes were beginning to swell with tears. Everything around me started to blur as a thumping in my ears made it feel like the room was reverberating. I climbed into the tub and cradled my knees to my chest. There was no way to organize my thoughts or define them or to think clearly. I just felt pressure all over my body, in my chest, and in my head, like I was going to burst from the inside out.

As the pressure in my body rose, my breathing constricted, and I gasped for air through my tears. I could hear faint cackling from the kitchen through the walls, and I just wanted to escape my house. I rocked in the bathtub for a long time, my skin against the cold, white porcelain, bouncing my mother's words around in my head, forcing myself to take short, quick breaths, trying to calm myself down.

I couldn't understand then why I was so upset. I couldn't articulate that my mother had reduced me to a small and empty trinket. I didn't know how deeply that would come to define how I saw myself. But I could feel it. Something inherently rose up from inside of me and was warning me about the inner storm I had brewing. Something violent and chaotic and dark was reaching for my mind, for my perception of myself and of the world around me, and my five-year-old body shivered with embarrassment that I was a dummy.

CHAPTER TWO
Silence

My father came quietly through the front door around three-thirty. My mother had already cleaned up the house from her day with the neighbors—they knew to leave before my father came home—and she was preparing dinner.

When he came in from work, everyone stayed out of my dad's way. He didn't speak to anyone and no one spoke to him. By four o'clock, my mother served him his dinner with a glass of water, a small tumbler of scotch, and the daily newspaper to the left of his plate. My sisters and I left the room with my mother, never bothering my father during his supper. After dinner, my father stood up and walked away from his plate to ready his things. I'd watch him from a distance, wondering about his life. Tonight, he would head out. My father seemingly always had a meeting or an event to attend—always vague in description—and if he didn't have anywhere to be, he worked on his properties in the neighborhood before taking a bath and heading to bed. He was always far away from us, even though we all lived in the same house.

On Saturday morning, I woke up before everyone else. After pulling my socks on, I tip-toed past my father's bedroom and into the bathroom. I could hear him shuffling papers in his room. He was awake, and already organizing his affairs. My father opened mail, dealt with finances, and seemed to centralize everything about his life in his tiny bedroom. It was where he slept and served as his private study. He was always up early, so I was careful not to let the floor creak as I scurried past.

When I came out of the bathroom, I could see my mother in the living room, curled up on the couch with blankets strewn across her. I shuffled quietly past her and to the refrigerator for a glass of milk. She turned with a small groan, opening up to the morning, before heading to the kitchen to start my breakfast.

I sat at the kitchen table with my glass of milk, fingering through the pile of mail. My mother gave me an angry look and mouthed the word "stop" to me so that I wouldn't get caught riffling through my father's mail. He was intolerant of having to explain to my mother that neither she nor the kids needed to be meddling in bills that we weren't paying. As she clicked on the stove burner, I heard my father. He was already halfway in the kitchen when he saw my mother shoo my hands away from the mail. Indirectly, he scolded me by telling my mother that I should know better than to touch his things. Like always, in a very passive-aggressive voice, "Yes, sir," my mother answered.

I spent the day outside with Emma Kay. There was a roofing company at the end of our street, and they had materials protected by high fences. Anything toxic was kept in rusted barrels that collected rainwater, creating a gross tar-like mixture of chemicals. Emma and I made a ritual of climbing the fences, though, taking some of the wood the company had piled.

"Careful," Emma whispered to me as I swung my leg atop the chain-link fence. I hushed her with a gesture. When I was on the other side, I carefully lifted pieces of wood over to Emma before making a stealthy exit. We laughed, looking at each other, running back down the street, our hands full of the stolen wood. The sun shone down on Emma's sandy brown hair, gleaming as it floated in the wind beside me. My hair was in two braids, matted to each side of my head. My hair didn't float at all—just stuck out unevenly on both sides.

We used the wood to build an outside fort, but we also did it because we knew we weren't allowed to. We climbed into the local scrap yard for supplies, and beyond that were railroad tracks where we found thousands of pieces of bound manila paper. We never knew what the paper was meant for, but we stole it to color on all of the time. Ultimately, our fort came to be made of wood, the manila paper, and a few blankets. We sat in our fort, coloring, sucking on popsicles, and talking most of the day away, before having to go back to our houses for dinner.

After dinner and once my father was gone, I watched my mother get ready for bingo. She went most nights of the week, and I liked to watch her smooth her hair and pull lipstick across her mouth in the mirror. At seven years old, I felt so close and so far away from womanhood. My mother was still a mysterious creature to me, unlike my sisters, three of which had moved out, leaving just me and Camille.

Camille was troubled. She wasn't happy. I didn't know then what type of help she needed, but I knew something was wrong with Camille. She was cruel to me, and I often feared my mother leaving because Camille was tasked with babysitting me. My heart started to beat faster as I watched my mother finish primping and collect her things before heading out the door to bingo.

For a short while, the house was quiet. I stayed in the bedroom while Camille was in our living room, on the phone, complaining about babysitting to her friends. It wasn't long before she hung up and I heard her stomping around, making her way into the bedroom. She was intentionally heavy-footed when she wanted to appear aggressive. You could feel the weight of her procession around the house, bringing destruction along with her.

I hurried into the bathroom and got in the tub. I needed the touch of the cold porcelain to help me steady my breathing. As Camille marched around the house, I was busy taking small, hurried breaths so that I wouldn't pass out. My heart beat quickly and I tried to keep the labor of it all quiet. While I didn't know what to call these episodes yet, my little body had gotten so used to panic attacks that I'd developed a routine. Cradling myself in the bathroom made me feel a little bit safer, and helped me calm down a little more quickly.

Camille swung the bathroom door open, ominous in her posture. In an instant, she'd broken my seal of safety, and my heart sank forcefully down into the pit of my stomach, making me feel sick with her presence.

"What the fuck are you doing?" she accused.

Meek and scared, I couldn't talk. The anxiety of it all was too amplified; the room pulsing around me. Camille didn't like being ignored. She was too used to being ignored by my parents, and she wouldn't be ignored by me while I was in her charge. She swayed over to the tub and sat on its ledge. I pulled my knees in tighter.

With piercing eyes, excited to hurt me, Camille often reminded me in harsh tones filled with the sting of heat, "I wish you were never born, you know. If mom hadn't spread her legs, you wouldn't be here at all."

My eyes narrowed as I looked back at Camille before turning away.

"Look at me, you little bitch!" she demanded.

But I didn't want to. I wanted to be left alone and I was scared of her. Our mother wouldn't be home for hours yet, and I could sit in the bathroom the rest of the night. Camille used these hours to exercise her power over me, to capitalize on my diminished stature.

When I wouldn't look at her, Camille pulled my head back and grabbed me by the throat. My legs dropped down and my hands struggled to push away Camille's arms. I wasn't strong enough to defend myself against her, and I knew from practice that I wouldn't be able to escape her grasp. Her goal was to see how long she could cut off my breathing before I passed out. We found out many times that it didn't take very long.

Mom and her friends were particularly quiet the next day. Their normal howls and cackles were replaced with hushed tones and serious sounds that seemed like warnings from my grandmother. I crept around them, hiding my wet sheets and changing my pajamas in the bathroom. I told myself I wouldn't drink anything that day. Mom was getting tired of me wetting my bed.

"Why did you get in?" my grandmother quietly scolded my mother.

"I didn't!" my mother retorted. "Hang on," Mom turned from her friends at the table, seeing me pass out of the corner of her eye. "What do you got there, Celia?"

I hurried into the bathroom without answering her.

"I swear, girl! I'm going to hang those sheets outside for everyone to see! Celia?"

Grandmother beckoned my mother to continue her story.

"She's so lazy! Just keeps peeing the bed instead of getting up!" my mother went on before turning back to her friends with a sigh and continuing, "After he slowed down beside me, he just opened the door and grabbed me. I've had them slow down and ask me to get in before, but he didn't even bother asking. I panicked, and by struggling, I was able to slip out of the car."

"You jumped out of the car?" my grandmother asked, her hands waving.

"I had to!" my mother declared.

"Same thing happened to Velma," a woman with tight curls, picking up her cigarette from the ashtray, chimed in. Everyone turned to look at her. "Yeah, Velma from right behind you. Said she was walking home from bingo, too, when a car pulled up next to her and the man grabbed her and pulled her in. She slipped out, too."

After consoling my mother, they all played the numbers for the latter part of the afternoon, and by the time my dad was coming through the door, my mother already had dinner piping hot. She didn't say anything to my father about her brush with kidnapping the night before, and it wasn't going to stop her from going to bingo tonight. Without a word, she served him his plate and then went to put on her makeup. I looked on at my mother as she brushed past me, over at Camille shoveling her dinner into her mouth, over at my plate next to hers, in front of an empty seat, over to my dad, sitting alone with his dinner and his scotch, reading the newspaper. Everyone had their own agenda, their own separate lives—everyone besides me. We moved and participated in a family without talking, without any sign of warmth, without any outward signs of love or communication.

The room felt cold, and something came over me unexpectedly. I felt my legs begin pushing forward, and I walked over to my father and interrupted his dinner. I wasn't sure what I wanted to say, but there was a lump in my throat that was trying to form some sort of meaning. I wanted to ask him a million questions about his life and about our life as a family and ask why he never talked. I wanted to tell him that someone tried to take Mom, but I just stared at him, chewing his food and sipping his scotch, the sound of it all reverberating. He noticed my feet in front of him and shuffled in his chair, surprised.

Putting down his papers, "What?" my father asked.

I didn't say anything, just stared.

My father rolled his eyes and uttered a low growl. He pursed his lips before opening them. With force, "What is it, Celia? Can't you see I'm eating? Is that difficult for you to see?"

My father never spoke too much—just enough to get his point across—and in those three sentences, I cowered away from him. He was upset at having to talk at all, and any time this happened, he treated all of us like we were the most stupid and intolerable people he had to deal with. If you had the nerve to ask him a question, his voice became deeper and louder to show his impatience and sheer disgust at having to look at you and use words to provide you with information.

"Don't talk to her like that," my mother snapped. I was surprised to hear her defend me, but we all regretted that she did.

Enraged, my father stood up from his dinner and began yelling at my mother with a booming voice that echoed off the walls. Camille got up from the table and went to the bedroom while I ran and hid behind the bathroom door, next to the hot water tank. I slid down and got low, kept myself as small and quiet as I could. I stayed there, crouched, until the argument was over, drowning out their words the whole time. Looking over at the bathtub, I shook the memory of Camille attacking me from my mind. I disconnected. I let my mind wander to other places. I left what was real for what I could imagine inside that bathroom.

I laid in bed that night, tossing, unable to steady my mind or my heart. I knew there had to be more out in the world, and instead of sleeping, I was living in a constant daydream. I heard my mother come in from bingo around ten-thirty, so I quietly slipped out of my bed and through the kitchen.

Mom was tired and full from gambling and walking the long way home, but she waved me over to come sit on the floor in between her legs so that she could braid the side of my head that had come loose. She asked me if I wanted her to pin-curl my hair.

"Yes!" I said. Excited, I ran and got the jar of bobby pins from the bathroom cabinet. My mother took my hair down, combed it, and began to place the pins.

I sat there quietly, thinking deeply in the dim light of the evening, my back pressed against the couch.

"Does my father love me?" I asked.

My mother looked down at me, stroking my hair, "Of course he loves you," she said.

"How do you know?"

She took a moment, and then said, "He loves you."

I was always confused by her responses, by the way she teetered between kindness and indifference. That's why I think I was so unsure about which things in the world were real and which things weren't. But I was even more perplexed by my father, although, at least he was consistent in his disdain for us. If the first and most important relationship you have with a man is the one you have with your father, I was in serious trouble. Between trying to decipher my parents' relationship and how my dad felt about me, I was left without a fundamental understanding of how relationships between men and women even work.

I turned to my mom one more time with another question burning on my lips.

"What is it?" she asked, softly and sleepy-eyed.

"I feel okay to watch myself when you're gone. I'd like to, actually, instead of having Camille babysit me," I kept my gaze on her face, studying her immediate reaction.

My mother was unsure, but she didn't debate it for long. "You sure?" she confirmed.

"Yes," I was stern.

"Okay then, go to bed."

I nodded at my mother as she stretched out onto the couch and pulled her blankets over her shoulders. Then I shuffled back to the bedroom and quietly into bed.

CHAPTER THREE
The Periphery

China dolls are beautiful and innocent, and at one point, so was I. But they are also fragile, easily broken, and all dressed up to sit on someone's shelf. China dolls wear the finest silk clothing and are glazed from the purest porcelain. I certainly wasn't wearing fine clothes, and no one was admiring me. When I was young, I didn't want to be a China doll. I didn't want to be as delicate as I was—as weak as my mother insinuated. But as I got older and became more aware of my body, I also realized that this nickname meant that I might be beautiful, and I clung onto that once I had to go to school.

At first, I was a pretty good kid in school, but I was surrounded by white students because the schools were outside of our neighborhood. By fourth grade, Emma Kay had moved away, so I didn't have her by my side. Her parents split up, Emma moved with her mother, placing her in some other school district, and her father moved over to Lagrange Street, just a few blocks away. At the time, I didn't know Emma's mother had also re-settled in the north end. She'd moved enough blocks away, though, that she'd gone out of my range. I never really ventured that far, and as a result, I lost touch with Emma.

But I made some new friends. As Emma moved away, Mary's family moved in, and we instantly became close. Mary grew up in a house with five other kids. They were poor, and they ate potatoes almost every day—potato soup, fried potatoes and onions, French fries. Mary wasn't allowed to play outside until her chores were done, and one of her chores was always cutting up the potatoes in preparation for a meal, but she would get in trouble if she cut too much of the potato away when she was peeling the skin. I used to help her so it would get done faster, but she had to teach me how to do it correctly. Hurriedly, we'd finish prepping the potatoes so we could meet up with two other neighborhood girls, Vidette and Noreen, at our club house.

Our club house was in Noreen's basement, with a door that opened from the ground outside from which we could crawl down into the basement and into our private club. We had one room of the basement for our clubhouse, and Noreen's brother, Ed, had the other for his boy's club. We painted the clubhouse, painted our names on the walls, and decorated it with old couches and tables.

For the first time in my life, my insulated borders expanded, and I had to leave the block five days a week for school. I walked from my poverty-stricken corner of town, over the train tracks and the bridge, where a few homeless people lived, to go to public school. The neighborhood kids waited for each other outside so that we could walk to school safely, together. Even though we walked together, the long walk to school gave me a sense of independence. There were many people from my neighborhood who would come to suffer an untimely death, but the first time I saw someone die was while walking to school with one of my classmates, Patrick.

On a back street, right before the train tracks, Patrick and I were talking. I'm not sure if Patrick was trying to impress me or others in the group, but he announced he was going to jump on the back of a passing semi before he took off running. Patrick jumped, lost his footing and fell, hitting the back of his head on the concrete. He died right there on the street, before the ambulance arrived.

As I stared at Patrick's body, I expected him to get up—not to be dead. I could see his body splayed about, his arms stretched out, his legs twisted, and the blood pooling under his head, but I couldn't push myself to believe he was dead. *What does that mean?* I'd seen other kids do so many stupid things—stunts they never thought about—and survive, so why hadn't Patrick survived? *Why did I always need to be vigilant? Why did Mom always warn me to keep my wits about me? Why did I know, deep inside, that I needed to stay sharp?* There were so many dangers around all of us all of the time, so I couldn't reckon with Patrick's death. It was too simple. Too stupid. I couldn't make sense of it, and I never quite moved past that stunned feeling. There was nothing to do other than to turn and walk to school.

That day in school, I sat quietly, contemplating, trying to find the lesson in Patrick's death, some meaning, thinking about how quickly it had all happened, wondering how his parents must feel. *Why did he decide to jump on that truck anyway?* I wasn't the only one who saw Patrick die, but the school didn't offer any of us grief counseling. They just expected us to deal with it.

Because I was such a social kid, I got in trouble most days for talking to my friends during class. My parents could always count on my report card having the same written note each quarter: "Celia talks too much to her neighbor," and, "If Celia spent more time on her studies rather than talking to her neighbor, she would have higher marks." But I was quiet the day Patrick died—stuck in my head, re-playing him jumping and falling, losing his life within a stretch of seconds. I perked up when I heard my name called over the intercom, packed up my books, and headed for the main office.

"Celia?" the attendant asked me over her glasses as I shut the office door.

I nodded.

"Come right over here, please." She ushered me in front of a baby blue backdrop, turned my body slightly to the side, and then positioned my chin forward over my shoulder. "Okay," she got behind the camera, "and smile!"

The photograph flashed and I blinked. The woman with the glasses thanked me and sent me back to class. I didn't ask any questions.

I had a lot of friends in elementary and junior high school, and I knew the teachers well. Even though I knew I looked different, my white friends and teachers acted like I was a part of the group. Once in a while, one of my peers made a racial jab or made fun of me, but I chased them down, both girls and boys, got a couple good licks in, and moved on. I was really tuned into the other kids' feelings, too. I never wanted anyone to feel bad or left out, and though I didn't always have the courage to speak up whenever I saw someone being bullied, I made sure to treat them kindly by talking to them whenever I saw them in school.

In a lot of ways, my differences made me feel special in the early grades. A couple of weeks after the attendant with the glasses took my picture, I walked into school to find my photo being displayed in the lobby as part of the district's diversity initiative. It didn't make me feel singled out. Instead, I beamed with pride and felt included. My picture was always in the glass case and usually on the front cover of every yearbook. *Me.* I felt different. Being different is good.

I strode through the front door of my house with a smile on my face that I'd carried home from school, but the dense presence of my father coming in behind me tore that away. I took my bookbag over to the kitchen table to empty out my papers when Camille trotted over and slammed her hand down in front of me. I followed her arm and looked up at her face.

"I'm going out with friends tonight. Mom says you can be alone now," Camille smirked at me. I could tell she was excited about the ruling.

I nodded at her, "That's right."

Camille chuckled at me before taking her dinner plate to the bedroom so she could get ready. Mom set my dinner down next to the stove and motioned for me to come pick it up while she served my dad at the kitchen table.

Everyone was out of the house by six-thirty. Camille went to a friend's house, my mother left for bingo, and my father went wherever he went. The house was quiet and dim with a fading evening sun. I was relieved to have some space to myself, to be free of the pressures of my family, free of the tension that kept me chained to Camille and to my anxiety. But it didn't last.

It wasn't long before I started to hear the sounds of my neighborhood—distant arguments, rolling laughter from other houses, people walking by on the street, the hum of cicadas with nightfall, and a terror fell over me. I was paralyzed with fear, and it was unexplainable. I thought my newfound independence from everyone would bring some relaxation, but as I wandered the house, looking for a comfortable place to rest, I grew more and more paranoid. My heart started the irregular beating I'd come to know so well, and my breath came in short and labored stints.

I found a tight corner in the living room that presented the best view of the house and slid my body down into a tight ball on the floor. I sat there for four hours, without television, alone in the silence, just listening for sounds. If anyone came into the house, I'd be able to see them right away, because my brain screamed danger. I had become so trained to fear the hours when my mother was away that I couldn't shake the feeling of impending disaster, even when I was all alone. I couldn't focus on anything other than trying to calm my mind, so I waited there until I heard my mother's heels clacking up the sidewalk towards the door. I waited for her to usher me to bed, knowing she'd be on the couch to keep watch.

When I stood up out of bed the next morning, the room immediately began to spin. I steadied myself against my bedpost and closed my eyes for a moment. I could feel myself losing the footing beneath me, but I took a deep breath and calmed a little. My head felt like it was full of air. When I opened my eyes again, the room was spinning even faster, and everything melded together like an impressionist painting of blurred colors. I couldn't see in front of me, so I traced the wall with my hand, leading myself to the bathroom, closing my eyes as much as I could on the way there. I noticed that if I held my head sideways that I could stave off the nausea, but not for long.

I stumbled into the bathroom and took a seat on the floor, next to the toilet, in case I did vomit. But after a few moments, I let myself lay down, pressing my cheek to the cold linoleum, and shut my eyes, trying to clear my mind. I heard footsteps in the kitchen outside the bathroom.

"Celia's sick, Mom!" Camille yelled.

My mother came to inspect me and I told her about the room spinning and that I couldn't move.

"She's just having another one of her spells," my mother confirmed to Camille, who I imagine rolled her eyes at this before pushing her way back into the bedroom.

My mother knelt down and felt my forehead, "You're cool, Celia."

"I feel like I'm going to be sick and I can't see," I whined to her.

My mother kept me home from school on the days of my "spells." The vertigo would last for hours at a time, but we never went to the doctor. The expense seemed unnecessary to my parents because dizziness wasn't life-threatening. It just became an undiagnosed condition that everyone came to expect.

That night, my mother arranged for Camille to babysit me. I'd gotten so tired of living in sheer terror when I was left home alone that dealing with Camille came to seem not so bad, and I especially needed a break after a day of feeling dizzy and nauseous. I'd confessed to my mother that I was afraid to be by myself, so she re-instituted my sister as babysitter.

We had a quiet evening, which was an enormous relief to my tired mind and body. Camille was busy talking to her friends and minding her business while I sat in the living room, doing my homework and watching television until my mother came home. I felt like we'd moved past our troubles and I chalked up her previous behavior to how confusing growing up can be.

When we settled into bed for the night, I had an ease in my heart, and I rested my foot on Camille's leg for comfort, drifting off to sleep. In an instant, I felt my face being hit with a forceful pressure that I couldn't breathe through. I couldn't open my eyes either. Camille had shoved a pillow over my face and was holding it down. I squirmed to release myself, but Camille pressed with all of her weight, trying to stop my breathing. Desperately, I kicked the wall as hard as I could for as many times as I could until my mother came in to yell at me. Hearing her yelling as she entered the bedroom, Camille let up and stopped.

I decided that night that I would go back to watching myself in the evenings—that I could never let my mother leave me alone with Camille again.

CHAPTER FOUR
The Boundary

I've always hated labels. And maybe that started with my mother calling me a China doll, but I hate the labels that people feel the right to assign to one another—the boxes that people feel pressured to fit inside of. It wasn't until junior high did I feel the pressure of a box shutting up around me. There was only one other black kid that had come to my school, and by the sixth grade, everyone thought he and I should date.

Even though I was horribly offended by the assumption that it was only fitting for me to date another black kid—the implication that I would automatically want to date him was weird—I was also trying to eke out my own personal identity. Being surrounded by white peers, that journey was isolating at times because it was more complicated for me than for the other kids. I started to think about who I *could* date and why, as well as who I *wanted* to date and why. I started thinking about my body and what other people thought about my body more, and none of this slowed down my panic attacks at home.

Outwardly, I was a gregarious girl with a lot of friends. I was accepted and fit in, despite the obvious racial differences between me and my peers. We laughed together, and everything was right with the world when I was with all of them. But inside, I didn't feel tenacious or cool or confident. I felt insecure and scared, and like I was starting to harden.

In seventh grade, I wrote a play that explored African-American cultural overtones. I modeled the main character after all of the strong older women in my family, creating an archetype that resulted in a character similar to Tyler Perry's Madea. In a twist that highlighted the intersection of race and the dominant culture, the main character presented as a witch who flew into town to help the townspeople. The school, in their never-ending endeavor to showcase cultural diversity among the students, put on the play, allowing me to cast my classmates.

At the end of the play, I received a standing ovation from a crowd full of white families. I scanned the audience for my mother and watched as her face contorted into amazement at the way everyone in the audience was laughing and enjoying themselves, and that they stood up when I came out onto the stage to take my bow. As a family who kept to our block, performing that play was the first time either of us had stepped outside of my mother's kitchen and experienced the embrace of others. I was developing a voice—an important one.

In the summer between seventh and eighth grade, a few years after an uprising by the Black Panther Party in Toledo and Detroit, they established a home for the Toledo chapter on Dorr Street and were evangelizing their message. Camille and her friends drove us up and down

Dorr Street, where young black people looking to show off their newly shined cars went to meet people. Seeing the Black Panther headquarters reminded me of the news reports from when the riots broke out. I saw fires and people yelling on the television, people throwing their fists in the air, fighting and moving through the streets of Toledo and Detroit. I remember my mother declaring that we'd move back to the country if the Black Panthers came too close to our street. In that moment, as we were riding down Dorr Street, I tried to piece together what my mother meant. I thought, *We're black, so why would the Black Panthers want to hurt us?* My mother was half white. *Does that mean that we aren't black enough?* I knew from being called a nigger over and over that I wasn't white enough to be called white. When we got home, I was still contemplating the Black Panther Party and my blackness.

"Celia," my mother called from the kitchen table, but I was sitting in front of the big box heater in the dining room, thinking about the world and my place in it, trying to piece together my understanding of these people who looked like me, marching through the city.

"Celia!" her tone hit a pitch I knew to answer, and I turned to meet her gaze. "Take this letter to the mailbox."

I careened out the front door and dropped onto the sidewalk. At thirteen, my mind was racing with questions. *Maybe the Black Panthers are right. Maybe it is time to put African-American rights on the forefront. Do my white peers think about being white? Do they feel limited by the color of their skin?* Everybody in my neighborhood was poor. Did middle class white people walk into neighborhoods like mine? *No. Maybe my family should join the Black Panther Party instead of being afraid of them.*

"Hey, girl," an old towncar with rust peeling over the wheel frames had pulled up next to me while I was dancing around in my thoughts. I stopped and meekly looked over, using mostly my peripheral vision. The man opened his car door. "Come on, want to get in?" he asked.

I shook my head no and fastened my pace. I could see the mailbox feet in front of me, but the man slowly rolled his car next to me, coaxing me to get in.

"You! Girl, come on," he continued. I didn't fully look at him. Instinctually, I knew I needed to escape the situation. Panicked, I started running and sprinted to the mailbox. I slipped the letter into the mailbox and took the corner at lightning speed, dashing between houses and back to my yard. I didn't stop to think about what might have happened if I'd gotten in the car. I told myself the world wasn't safe for girls like me and there was nothing I could do about it. I just went into my house and sat down for dinner.

There was no reason to tell anyone. I thought these kinds of things happened to everyone. I knew they happened to my mother and our neighbors, so I just knew that all women and girls needed to expect it from time to time. There were predators that wanted to hurt women and girls. I simply learned that I should be wary of drowning in my thoughts when I'm outside—I learned to be more vigilant.

By the time high school came, I was exploring my blackness with vigor, picked my hair out into an afro, read about the black power movement with veracity, and wrote "BLACK POWER" on all of my school notebooks. I was enthralled, and I felt part of something bigger than myself—something that represented me when no one else seemed able to. If there was power in the world to be had, I was going to seek it out.

That power didn't seem to lay in school. I was very smart, and I knew it, but it didn't stop the system from keeping me small and largely unseen. While I was used as the face of diversity in my white elementary school, that notoriety didn't seem to carry much weight in any other aspects of life. As I got older and graduated high school, the deafening presence of racism and exclusivity was overwhelming, and the more I studied, the more I noticed it—the more I realized we'd been conditioned to accept exclusion and abuse.

We traveled five miles outside of our neighborhood to go to high school. We walked four blocks to catch the bus to go "out Stickney," meaning we had to travel to a neighborhood that was even farther north than us, so we went out Stickney to school. I traveled to school with Mary and Vidette most days, and eventually, we started taking our time, catching the later bus if we had to. We'd heard about kids smoking weed, and we knew about smoking and drinking because of our parents, but we hadn't figured out a way to try more than smoking cigarettes yet. I'd stolen a couple of cigarettes from my mom and handed them to my friends.

With all of the discovery that comes with adolescence, we were all becoming more and more aware of where we lived, how we lived, and how different we were from our peers in high school. We lit up our cigarettes and waded through an old factory lot next to the marsh, short-cutting our walk to the bus stop.

"Look here," Vidette called out to us. She was crouched down by the edge of the marsh, fingering some green growth on the ground. We crowded around her, squinting. "I think it's weed," she questioned.

"No," I chuckled, and then looked at the leaves more closely. "Is it?" I stood back up.

Mary shrugged her shoulders. None of us knew what weed really looked like, but we all knew you were supposed to smoke it. Vidette started to pluck the plant from the ground.

"Here," I said, motioning for her to hand the "weed" to me. "If it is, let's see." I took out a cigarette from my pocket and gently rolled it between my fingers, emptying the tobacco out. Then I pulled apart the plant, stuffed it into the empty cigarette, and lit it. Mary and Vidette's faces lit up.

"Oh shit," Mary said, excited we were actually smoking weed.

We weren't. Whatever actual weeds Vidette had pulled burned up when I lit them and emitted a sticky residue that made the cigarette paper wet and gummy. I spit the cigarette out of my mouth and crushed it onto the ground. We laughed at each other, and finished our walk to the bus.

High school was a lot different than elementary and junior high. My elementary and junior high school was old. The center of each stair in the school dipped dramatically from years of wear. The windows were about four feet wide and bare, without screens. When it was hot, the teacher would open a window and a cool breeze flew into the room, scattering everyone's papers. I loved sitting in the breeze, letting the fluidity of the cool air wrap up and around me.

When awards were given, I could always count on taking home two or three for reading, comprehension, and spelling. I didn't have to try very hard in school, and I wasn't searching for anyone to make me feel "smart" either. I didn't need teachers or grades or principals or anyone legitimized by society to determine which of us is smart and not smart to validate me. I knew I was smart. I knew I picked up on information quickly, that I could quickly ingest different concepts, that I was absorbing things more deeply than my classmates—that I was keenly aware of the subtle nuances in their voices, in their perspectives, in the lessons I was being taught.

But something shifted in high school. It was a large place. I couldn't relate anymore. It was clear that the white kids bussed in from Point Place were valued by the school. They ran the student council, organized dances, and were the only ones picked to be cheerleaders for the school teams. They seemed to always smell good, chatter up and down the halls to each other, and always seemed happy. As excited as I was to have more access to my black people, my light skin tone, my semi-straight hair, and more proper language kept me at bay with them. And all of a sudden, being smart wasn't enough for my teachers.

I became aware that I lay outside of all that counted at school and that the people in charge weren't interested in people like me. I was a girl without a country—without a group to belong to and a place to fit in. I went from the star student, shining example of cultural diversity, to an invisible outcast overnight. I felt labeled, chided, secluded, and alone. It felt like everyone was looking at me, but no one was seeing me, and I railed against all of it with anger and reproach. In the turn of a year, I disengaged from the process of education completely. I resisted what resisted me, and I let go of any fantasy of a successful social life. I only nodded at the couple of kids I passed in the hallway who were from my neighborhood, Mary, Vidette, and Noreen—all scurrying quietly to their next class. Eventually, all of the kids from my neighborhood—all of them—would disconnect and quit high school. I would be the only one from my neighborhood to graduate, and it was only because I was too afraid to tell my father I wanted to quit.

In tandem with my rising sense of displacement, the feeling of segregation, in tenth grade, I found a dying black boy lying on his back in the middle of the street. His leg was twisted behind him, and his face was draining and blank. He was young, like me, and as he came into view upon my approach, when I realized what I was looking at, I froze at the curb. I watched as cars drove around him. No one did anything for a long time. I just stared. The scene didn't fit anything I knew about the world and about people yet. Life could be tough, and I'd seen death, but this was grotesque, and my fifteen-year-old brain didn't know how to compartmentalize such morbid neglect. *Why isn't anyone helping him?* My stomach turned over and my hands fell onto my knees. Finally, someone called the police, and as sirens sounded nearer, I felt utterly powerless looking into that boy's lifeless face.

I walked right past my family at home that night, silently. We'd all fallen into a quiet complacency that was easier than fighting, or feeling. My father came and went as he pleased, and once I'd grown through puberty and into a woman's body with a woman's mind and cognizance, I knew where he was going all of the time. I understood the look on my mother's face—the riff of shame that furrowed in her brow, giving her reason to sleep on the couch every night. I could place the floral smells wafting from his clothes in the late hours as he plummeted into the house and into his bedroom. I could hear the quiet sighs of dry tears from my mother. I had nothing to give them, though, and my father had never given me anything in the first place, so I sauntered around my parents, through our worn and emptying house, living solely in the land of my thoughts.

My parents never divorced despite it all. They didn't seem to love each other much, and with all of my sisters gone now, the three of us lived separate lives. We didn't go anywhere together. We didn't eat dinner together, even on Thanksgiving, because there was little to show gratitude for. I didn't belong to any extracurricular clubs or intramural sports, so there weren't any functions for my parents to attend on my behalf. We didn't celebrate Christmas together. We walked and moved in the same house, in parallel universes, orbiting each other with wide berths, ensuring there was never a collision. When I needed something for school—a notebook, a pen, something for an art project—I left my father a note. If I needed money, I knew to catch my father while he was reading the paper. I'd stand silently in front of him, wait for him to finish the section he was reading, peer over the paper at me, and hand me a dollar out of his shirt pocket. Often, he'd peer over the paper and say, "No," and that was it. I'd walk away. Negotiation required conversation and feelings, and I had learned the risk wasn't worth it.

We spoke when my mother told me we'd be going to visit one of my older sisters, Carmenita. Carmenita lived across the street from our house in one of my father's apartments, and being so much older than me, I never knew her very well. But I did know that she worked a lot. She worked for the things she wanted, I admired that about her, and she always bought me things when she could. Not only did she buy things for me, she would occasionally buy things my mother needed. She had been living with a guy from Detroit named Terry for some time, and while my mother and Carmenita were out picking out a new kitchen stove, Terry offered to take me bowling. He knew this would score points with my sister.

I was blindsided when Terry attacked me in the car after bowling. He put the car in park and tried to force his body on top of mine in the passenger seat. I scrambled for any escape, but he was much stronger than me, almost covering my small frame. I fought him as he put his mouth on me, and as he tried to push his body fully onto me, I bit his shoulder deeply before squirming out from under him and out of the car. As I stumbled to stand and started to make my way home on foot, Terry begged me not to tell. He pleaded with me to get in the car and let him drive me home. He promised not to try anything again. I got back in the car. I didn't tell anyone.

I believed it was my fault for not understanding that this might happen.
People take advantage of others when they're vulnerable.
Don't let your guard down.
Don't be vulnerable.
It's not safe for girls here

CHAPTER FIVE

Beyond the Veil

"You remember what I told you?" my mother asked me twice to repeat the directions to her. It was my first time traveling to the mall by myself and she was nervous about it.

"Eight blocks south to downtown, and then catch the 31H bus to Southwyck Mall at the Jackson Street stop. Got it."

It took a half hour to walk downtown from my house, and then another half hour for the 31H to show up. From there, the ride to the mall was about an hour long. I left early in the morning so that I'd have time to get to the mall, shop, and get back home before dark. I couldn't walk home alone in the dark.

I didn't really have money to spend at the mall spare a few dollars that I'd saved from my dad, but getting to travel there was a celebration of my budding independence. I liked to window shop—to marvel at the beaded dresses and the latest fashions. I watched mothers and daughters carting bags around the aisles, chatting with one another, comparing jeans and sizes. I went into little boutiques and fingered delicate earrings on the racks, telling each shopkeeper that I was "just looking."

> *As I perused, I thought about my own mother—about all of the jewelry she refused from my father, about her lipstick, about her pain. About her baking a peach cobbler pie. I thought about her smoking cigarettes at the kitchen table, running numbers and cracking jokes; a cackle-filled room of hens, separate from the rest of the world, from this world. I thought about Emma Kay. The boundaries of my neighborhood didn't glitter like the things in the mall stores, and it was much brighter in the mall than my streetlights could shine. But I liked to think about my mother and I walking the stretches of these stores, trying things on, using credit cards, and smiling at each other.*

I watched the other kids with their friends or their parents, loitering on the weekend. I bought a fountain soda and sat inconspicuously in the food court, just out of their range of attention, watching them flirt and fold with laughter. Their skin shimmered in the parting sun from the skylights, and I knew I could never be like them. I could go the same places, like the same things, but I could never mingle in their crowd—could never spend an afternoon at the mall with them—and there was an anger growing inside my gut, flowering into a rot that was tangled up inside of me.

I hadn't felt anxious or like my breath was being taken away from my body in a long time. Now I just felt strange. My longing morphed into intense anger. I realized that it wasn't just the world outside of my immediate neighborhood and my school that rejected me. I realized I was left out of everything! This wasn't like my longing to be the beautiful white people I watched on television, because, somewhere in my mind, even though I longed for my family to be like the Waltons or the Brady Bunch, I knew this was a fantasy, a make-believe world designed to make you think others lived as beautifully as you wouldn't. But the beautiful people were here, at the mall. This was happening in real life right before my very eyes. The people in my neighborhood were so poor. We couldn't buy these things. Our clothes were not as nice. Our smiles weren't bought and paid for, imperfect. Our shampoo didn't make our hair look luxurious.

The clouds waded across the sun, dulling the light in the food court, and checking the time, I realized I had already stayed longer than I meant to. I rushed to the bus stop and rode the 31H back into downtown Toledo, and from there I'd walk the rest of the way home, chasing the setting sun.

I stepped off the bus and started down the sidewalk, but I had spent too long at the mall. The evening was upon me, the daylight had dimmed into a cool darkness, and I started to walk as quickly as I could, keeping note of my surroundings the whole time. I was scared to walk home in the dark, and knew that nighttime in my town brought out terrors that were different from those in the daylight.

Three blocks down and I was approaching a man ahead, stumbling around the sidewalk, his back to me. He had a long grey duster that was tattered and dancing in the wind behind him. His pants had large stitched holes, and the rest of his body was amorphous from a distance—a large, dark blob floating around the sidewalk. I fastened my pace, hoping to just cut around him quickly and continue my trek home, but as I came upon him, he veered around quickly. Startled, I fumbled backwards, and when I looked down, the man was exposed, with an erect penis protruding from his pants. He was masturbating and looking at me.

Terrified, I looked away and darted across the street without checking for cars, and sprinted for as far as I could. I'd come to understand much later in life that my zip code was one of many poverty-stricken neighborhoods where parole and probation officers guided their sex-offending clients to live. My neighborhood had ten times the number of sex offenders than any middle class neighborhood in my city.

With fear still tingling in my body, I slowed down to a walk once I was near my house so that I could catch my breath. I hit Cherry Street and was more familiar with the rest of the way home. To be sure, I looked back over my shoulder, checking that the man hadn't followed me. That's when I saw Emma Kay.

I had heard some rumors about her. I thought I'd heard my mother whisper some wild and unbelievable things to her friends about Emma, but I hadn't seen her since she moved away years prior, and what I saw scared and saddened me.

By thirteen, Emma Kay was smoking weed and hanging out with older people in the neighborhood. I knew that. She'd stopped going to school, and I heard that Emma frequently wandered off for days at a time. As much as her mother tried, she was overwhelmed with the care of her many other children and a failing marriage. Emma moved in and out of her mother's house over the years, but little did I know, that just a few blocks away from me, Emma had been trafficked into the sex trade when she was just fifteen years old. To cope with the trauma of being trafficked, Emma had become addicted to crack cocaine, and her life revolved around seeking and smoking the drug. She wasn't interested in anything else, and I lost knowledge of her as my life moved on, oblivious about what had happened to her.

Seeing her on Cherry, I could see that Emma had given up. She was a gaunt and hollow version of my childhood friend, sauntering down the sidewalk. She looked tired, defeated, her eyes buzzing and sunken, and at the time, I didn't understand what was wrong with her. All I could see was a person I missed, but didn't know anymore.

I turned back quickly, trying to piece my feelings together, and kept walking toward home. It was too much to see Emma Kay that way, and after all that had happened throughout the day, I needed to get into my house—I needed to feel safe.

When I told my mother about the man, she told me that I shouldn't walk alone anymore. I nodded and went to my room, lying down on my bed and into a deep contemplation. I knew I wanted more in life than what was being offered to me. Nothing seemed safe. Nothing seemed whole. Nothing made me happy. I knew that the way the world looked at me, the way it treated me, wasn't how I wanted to be seen or treated. I was more than that. I wasn't meant to be kept small and scared and angry. But I was the only one that saw anything in myself—I was seemingly the only one who could see and feel what others couldn't: that

I had real potential, and a purpose bigger than all this.

I met Michelle senior year—the same year the school system had identified me as a prime candidate for their H.E.R.O. program, which stood for Home Economic Related Occupations. The goal of the program? For me to go out and get a job. I reported to one classroom for the entire day with the sole focus of finding a "fitting" position in the food industry that offered a wage I could at least feed myself on.

As a poor black kid, the school assumed that I needed to be helped out of a cycle of welfare. They assumed because I didn't talk much that I didn't have anything to say. They assumed because of my circumstances that I wasn't smart enough for, or capable of, higher education. But the opportunities they presented to me were well below my capacity, and as opportunity is connected to expectation, it would have been easy for me to fall into the belief that I wasn't worth more than a minimum wage job. And for a time, part of me did question my worth, but never my intelligence.

Though I didn't attend school regularly and barely made Cs, the school had no idea that I was smart—smart enough to calculate how many times I could miss school before they would call home, smart enough to sign in late, be counted as present, and then leave out the opposite door, and smart enough to attend classes once a week so I could gain a basic understanding of the content in order to pass classes with at least a C or a D.

Not only did the H.E.R.O. club turn me off, but there were bullies in the program, specifically a set of twin girls that teased me and called me names. They got under my skin so badly, and I used to fantasize about them finding themselves in a vulnerable situation where I could make them feel terrible about themselves. I wanted them to feel like outcasts, too. I wanted to have the same power they had over me.

I stopped in to visit my school counselor and asked for the catalog for the local university. The counselor looked up my transcript. Taking a serious tone, the counselor advised me to try and apply to a local factory. He told me that the H.E.R.O. club was only going to get me as far as working in a fast food restaurant or help me to understand how to spend my food stamps wisely, but getting a job at some place like the Jeep factory would give me a livable wage and something that I could raise a family on. I saw the University of Toledo catalog on his bookcase, but I didn't see him move toward retrieving it. I told him thank you as I left.

I got a job quickly, like the school expected me to. I interviewed at Burger King and was immediately hired. I worked there for three months and hated every second of it, and I wasn't about to capitulate some racist and classist cycle the school system thought I was a part of by staying there. I had my cousin write a letter to the program explaining that I was working for his company and would be preoccupied with my budding profession. I spent the rest of the year hanging out with my friends, including Dana and her sister, Jessie.

Dana lived around the corner from me. Her family moved in when I was sixteen, and she was quickly inducted to my group of friends. Together, we snuck out to drink, and we smoked weed and cigarettes at my house while my mother was at bingo. Being drunk and high quieted the questions swirling in my mind and took the anxiety and anger away. Dana had an older sister and lived in a single parent home. We all went to the same high school together, but Dana was not an intricate part of our neighborhood group, and that was of her own choosing. I wanted to be closer friends with Dana, and I'd go over her house in an effort to build a closer relationship with her, but Dana was often out spending time with a lot of other people. We were close enough, though, to occasionally skip school together.

I went to school once a week, to check in, but when I wasn't at school, I was over someone's house drinking beer and playing cards all day. Drinking and smoking became my new pastime, and my new circle of friends revered me for being so good at both. I loved the escape of it all. None of it felt dangerous, rather all of it made me feel happy and wanted. Being intoxicated reinvigorated my feelings, made me feel light and fun and carefree. It was liberating in a way that I had never experienced before, and all of the feelings that I had stuffed and caged deep inside of me felt even further away when I was inebriated.

Seeing what was going on, my mother started calling me "the ring-tailed leader," which was a label that represented power and I wore it with pride. For the first time, everyone was listening to me. Everyone was following my lead, and after a lifetime of fear, anxiety, and shame, I perverted that power to make myself feel happy, thinking I was strong and that being popular was the best thing that had happened to me yet. And the drugs. The drugs made me feel like the queen.

It wasn't long before I ran into trouble. There were rumors that a woman in her twenties named Vickie had it out for me. It had to do with us sharing the same boyfriend, but at different points in time, and now she thought I wanted him back. As a warning, Vickie had already stabbed my friend, John, causing him to need 137 stitches. She was serious. And she wasn't after a fist fight. Vickie was ready to draw blood.

In a panic, I explained to my mother the trouble I was in, and word had it that Vickie had just broken into another girl's house and beaten her pretty badly. My mother, impatient and wanting to leave for bingo, walked me into my father's bedroom and opened the top dresser drawer. She pulled out a box and opened it gently.

"This is a .22," my mother said. "Shoot the girl if she comes into this house."

I stared at my mother, wide-eyed, and swallowed. With that, she shoved the box back into the closet, picked up her purse, and left for bingo.

I was walking up the steps of my house, coming home from my weekly check-in at school, when my mother ran out onto the porch, yelling for me to hear.

"Michelle died!" my mother wailed.

I looked up at her, puzzled, unsure of what she'd said. "What?" I stopped and met her on the porch.

"Michelle. She was raped and killed by a cab driver," my mother exclaimed with her hands. "Jeanie came over and told me this morning."

"What?" I said again, eyes widening as this information settled into my brain.

My mother came close to me and pounded on my chest with her fist, "She was stabbed in her chest and she's dead."

Staring, I couldn't believe what she was telling me, and I couldn't process how insensitive her delivery was. I felt the pounding of her fist on my chest and an anxiety rise up from my stomach. I pushed my mother's hand away and walked past her, into the house. The pounding on my chest woke up the anger and frustration I had inside of me.

"People die, Ma! Girls die! And who cares? No one. People hate you because of the color of your skin. People hate you because you're poor. Your life means nothing. Men rape and kill women, and no one cares," I exploded, yelling.

I wore my bravado until I made it to my bedroom. There, I cried. All of the pain flooded in. Michelle was a nice Arab girl with long black hair. *Why would someone hurt her?* She was a kind soul. I hated the entire world. Lying there for hours, I started to think about Emma, about Patrick, and about the boy who died in the street, the man that wanted me to get in his car, my mother being grabbed into a car, my sister's boyfriend, the sexual pervert masturbating while staring at me. I thought about my panic attacks, my broken heart, and it all finally started to become painfully clear.

My mother wasn't just a cruel woman,

and my sisters weren't simply bullies,

My sisters and my mother knew something the whole neighborhood knew:
Life is harsh for poor kids. Dangers lurk.
My mother knew she couldn't be there every time a tragedy occurred.
Weakness was not allowed in this environment. ***Weakness doesn't survive.***
She couldn't shield me from the harsh realities of rape, death, and the coldness of an uncaring, unempathetic world.
I'm sure my mother couldn't have articulated it,
but in the back of her mind,
she was attempting to create a strong child
and a strong woman that could withstand the realities of hood life.
Murder happens, people die, and life is cruel.
Toughen up or run the risk of not making it.
Life is full of predators and prey.

Michelle was the first, but she wouldn't be the last. We had to learn to be hypervigilant, to watch out for ourselves. While the kids at the mall probably worried about passing their SATs or about what they would wear to the prom, by seventeen, I already knew what death looked like and had barely escaped several attempted sexual assaults.

CHAPTER SIX
Gaining Grit

After Michelle's death, I hardened with a toughness that felt safe. Though I was a kind, creative, funny, and a gentle person on the inside, there was no room for that in my neighborhood. I pushed all of that down, and, in its place, a rage brewed inside of me that spawned uncontrollable behavior. I was angry. And it probably wasn't just Michelle's death that birthed my anger. It was a conglomeration of my entire life. It had all been too much, and by the time I was seventeen, I could either break down or harden up. I hardened, and I became the stereotype—the young person that people expect to meet from neighborhoods like mine.

I got tired of being the prey and decided to become the predator. I wasn't a fragile China doll, but I wasn't truly that hardened bitch you don't want to meet in a dark alley either. I had the verbal threats down pat and I could appear scary and intimidating. My words and my tone could cut anyone down to size, but I was too small for any physical violence. I used my brain to calculate danger, and later my gun to equal the playing field. I understood how to navigate dangerous neighborhoods and how to negotiate power. I had given up knowing I was smart and doing something about it, like going to college. I hated my father. I hated my mother. I hated my neighborhood and the whole stupid charade. I especially hated society and the bullshit perpetuated about fairness and pulling yourself up by your bootstraps. There was no such thing like that for people in my neighborhood. I stayed high when I could, drinking and smoking weed to pass the time away.

Love in the hood is not always kind, sweet love. Saying to your girlfriend, "Hey, big head, what are you getting into tonight?" is not an insult, but an endearing comment. If you like someone, you throw in compliments with insults because if you can laugh together while maintaining your edge, you can bond with someone and be best friends or lovers. This type of talk is highly inappropriate in the middle class world—something some of us learned the hard way.

In our senior year, Mary met a guy from a middle class family who seemed really nice. They fell in love and took pictures together with Mary wearing an engagement ring. This was a huge deal to us all because it seemed like at least one of us was going to escape the neighborhood and live some semblance of a middle class life. When the boy's mother found out about Mary, though, the relationship was over.

People in my world didn't interact with people in the middle class world in any meaningful way. Every entrance was blocked. We went to schools that poorly prepared students. Our education only afforded my friends poor paying jobs—jobs that would never offer a living wage—

and none of us were prepared for college upon graduation. We had poor housing with asbestos, lead paint, and other environmental hazards that threatened our health. We only had access to partners that couldn't afford to take care of their families and were socially, psychologically, and physically blocked from access to more financially successful and eligible marriage partners. Negligent police responses to violence caused higher levels of trauma and reactions to trauma. We had no bootstraps with which to pull ourselves up.

After the broken engagement, Mary drifted away from us again, but I found out that she'd gotten a job as a dancer in a strip club. I'm not sure how it happened. Mary would stop by occasionally and we'd share a beer, but we were no longer close. Things had changed. All of sudden, Mary had grown up so fast, and she was working in a world that I wasn't familiar with. We couldn't connect, and though she'd stop by and we were friendly, she wasn't my friend anymore. I didn't know Mary anymore. Over time, Mary and I lost touch completely.

We were all nearing real adulthood, trying to figure things out. Some of my friends seemed to have fallen victim to things I didn't understand, some seemed to have just disappeared, and the rest of us felt caught in limbo, with nothing else to do other than get high together.

My parents finally separated and my father moved into one of the houses that he owned across town. None of my friends graduated high school—not one of them. I decided to become a drug dealer because those were the jobs that were plentiful and available in my neighborhood.

When I was nineteen, my mother decided to take one of the only two long distance trips that she would take in her entire life. She was going to California to visit her brother. She asked me to collect a check from my father for her and walk it downtown to her bank. As soon as my father dropped the check off, I cashed it. If you know people, you can cash any check in the hood as long as it's good, regardless of whether your name is on it or not. I bought a pound of weed, weighed it out, and bagged it up.

I was so proud that I had finally found my niche in life that I had a party to celebrate. I invited all of my friends from the neighborhood and friends from a few neighborhoods over. I hid the weed in my closet and we had a big party. I woke up the next day, ready to start my business, but the weed was gone. Every single bud was missing. I called my friends and questioned them about what may have happened. We went over the entire night, step-by-step. We narrowed thr suspect down to my boyfriend at the time, Rico. He stole my weed.

Of course, hood justice dictates that I threaten him or worse. I decided to threaten him. I wasn't a killer. I told him that I had a gun and would shoot him if he didn't return my weed. I had some of my guy friends stand outside his house while I told him on the phone that they would kill him, but I hadn't told them anything remotely like that. They thought they were on the lookout to see if he left. Rico agreed to meet me in an alley near the school bus stop to give me my weed back. He was scared and told me to come alone.

I was scared to go alone, so I promised him that I would come with my friend, Mr. .44 Magnum. In reality, I couldn't afford such a gun, but in the hood, this is sometimes the way to receive justice. I showed up in the alley, without a gun, without any back up, facing a man much larger than I was. I could only hope that he believed I was as scary as I had bragged about on the phone or this could be the end of me.

Rico showed up alone. He was visibly shaken and maybe somewhat remorseful having stolen from his girlfriend. He had some of my weed with him. He admitted he smoked some and he sold some. In addition to some weed and some money, he gave me some acid he'd traded for, saying I could sell the few pills he had and get some of my mother's money back. We parted ways for the last time.

I hit Lagrange Street, first selling the weed and then the acid. I still didn't have enough money to put back in my mother's account. I was fifty dollars short, so I came up with a plan. I would sell my friend's birth control pills up and down Lagrange Street, passing them off as double dome THC, which was the hot drug at the time. I sold them for three dollars a hit until I made up the fifty bucks. I raced the money down to the bank and made it just in time before my mother's plane touched down. Not only did I put my own life at risk, I put my friend at risk for pregnancy, sold "dummies," or fake drugs, to people I knew on the street—a crime that may not go unanswered—and I went from selling weed to issuing threats and harder drugs in less than twenty-four hours. Things spiraled out of control quickly and easily. I didn't have a choice but to follow the only path that seemed ahead of me.

I grew more paranoid as time passed, trying to wager who I'd become, negotiating which path in life I'd pursue. I was close to the edge. After getting really high with everyone at my house, Dana wouldn't stop talking. I looked over at my boyfriend and he could see the growing frustration in my eyes. It was an irrational anger, but an anger nonetheless, and as Dana continued to ramble, I went and grabbed that gun in the bedroom drawer. Marching back into the living room, I pulled the gun out and pressed it against her head. She stopped talking.

For a moment, everyone in the room yelled at me in shock to put the gun down, but I flashed them all a warning look. I told Dana how she was getting on my nerves, that I couldn't take her talking anymore. She was shaking at the end of the barrel. Everyone convinced me to put the gun down. Angrily, I marched into the bedroom and put it back in the box, and almost everyone quietly left. But sometimes, I think back at that anger in aghast. What would have happened had I pulled that trigger?

The only people left were Jeri and my boyfriend, Joe. Jeri passed a joint to me as we sat on my living room floor, listening to music. My mother was still at bingo and we had the house to ourselves for the evening. I was startled to hear the phone ring, and even more startled by the frantic words coming from the other end.

"Vickie's coming now. She just finished fighting some girl in her front yard," the girl on the other end scrambled for her words. "She was going to stab her, but she lost the knife in the grass. She's on her way to your house now."

I hung up the phone. Before I could make my way out of the back door, Vickie kicked the front door in, and the sound of the wood breaking off its hinges was thunderous. She saw Jeri first, ran to her, and banged her head on my mother's kitchen table. I watched in disbelief as Vickie threw Jeri's body around like a ragdoll. Vickie grabbed Jeri by the hair and flipped her over the back of the kitchen table chair. Once free, Jeri scrambled under the table, and Vickie turned to me.

Vickie was both tall and stocky, and I was ninety-five pounds soaking wet. My heart dropped and took my breath away. I stared at her, knees bent, ready to try and dodge her attack.

"You fucking bitch," Vickie rally cried before charging me. As she neared me, my boyfriend ran out from the bathroom and tackled Vickie from behind, pinning her down on the floor. He held her there while she screamed and writhed until she calmed down. Once she did relax, he let her up and stood between us. I stared at her face over his shoulder.

"I'll get you one day, bitch," Vickie pointed at me past my boyfriend, and then turned and left.

I knew I needed help, so I called on Camille to settle the score for me. And she did.

Camille put me in the car, drove straight to Vickie's house and had me point to her door. Camille laid on the horn of her car. Vickie opened the window of her upstairs duplex, perhaps hoping it was one of her many admirers.

Camille yelled up to her, "You got a problem? I heard you had a problem." Camille had a reputation for being the one woman that you don't want to mess with.

Finally realizing what this was all about, Vickie let my sister know that there was never a problem. "Oh no, Camille. Why? No, there is no problem."

My eyes were wide with fear that turned to pride. I was proud of my sister. Camille got out of the car to let Vickie know that she had something for her if there was a problem. Vickie reassured my sister that this was all a misunderstanding and that there wouldn't be a problem in the future.

Camille moved across town, and I was excited to see her new house. As I grew older, we became pretty close friends. After everything, I was packed and happy to stay with her that night, but I hated her live-in boyfriend, CJ. I never knew his government name. Camille and I spent the late evening catching up at her table without CJ ever bothering us, but I could feel his presence in the home and it made me uneasy. At the end of the evening, I covered the couch with a sheet and made a bed for myself.

A tingling pressure on my legs woke me up in the middle of the night, and I found CJ moving his hands up my thighs, trying to get under the covers with me. Jolted, I jumped and sat up, asking him what he was doing. CJ didn't say anything. Instead, he moved in and tried to kiss me. I backed up on the couch until my back was pressed against the armrest, but CJ continued to pursue me. He grabbed onto my breasts and pressed himself against me. Unwilling to be his victim, I protested and told him I would leave, that I would walk home and that I would tell Camille what he'd done. CJ moved back at that, stopped, and went back to my sister's bedroom. I was rattled.

Nervous, I laid there, awake and scared, mortified at the thought of having to confess what had happened to Camille. I spent the night mulling it over, and ultimately, I chose not to tell her. Camille had a volatile personality—this was the sister who had physically and emotionally tortured me as a young girl, and we'd come so far since then—so I was afraid that she would blame me for what CJ had done, that she would scream at me.

I chose to stay quiet.

In the morning, I simply asked her to take me home. I never stayed there again.

CHAPTER SEVEN
Walking Away

The north end of Toledo is not a place for the weak. While much of the world views communities like the one I grew up in as breeding grounds for bad people, the reality is that these places harbor a lot of good-hearted and intelligent people, especially women, who have been broken down and psychologically dissected by poverty, violence, and circumstance. As a result of economic segregation, the classist oppression of the poor creates an instinctual fire inside these people. Women mostly know that they and their children must be aware of the dangers around them. They know they must remain hypervigilant so they aren't taken advantage of or hurt.

There likely isn't anyone in north Toledo who hasn't been subjected to some sort of abuse, be it physical, emotional, psychological, or a combination of them all, and the hardening that results from this abuse is worn like armor. It's the shield that keeps these communities functioning—the understanding that links residents together. And with abuse comes exploitation.

As long as there are vulnerable bodies and minds, people will continue to be exploited, and this exploitation lives on a continuum that is important to understand. In many ways, the abuse that I endured growing up, both from within my family and from society, created a hardened exterior that protected me from exploitation. That abuse created a shell, something everyone in my neighborhood needed to survive, and while it might have also insulated some of my gifts for a time, it kept me safe. Members of poor and oppressed communities who can't navigate their environment and don't have any solid family support fall prey to severe abuse and exploitation, as I would come to find out.

Dana and her sister, Jessie, were home alone a lot. Often times, when their mother was at work, all the kids in the neighborhood would go over their house to hang out, drink, and play cards. But they'd been visiting an older African-American man's house when their mother was home and they wanted to skip school, and they'd asked me to come with them this time.

The man let us drink and smoke cigarettes in his house. He handed out smokes to all of us. Dana and Jessie had clearly been there many times before as they took it upon themselves to open his refrigerator and help themselves to whatever they wanted. At first, I thought this was cool, because in my neighborhood, if you didn't have any money to throw in on beer then you couldn't have any. But this guy didn't seem to ask the girls for anything, yet they could have whatever they wanted.

We sat around his kitchen table, casually swigging our beers, puffing on cigarettes, when Dana went over to the man and sat on his lap.

It caught me by surprise, and I had difficulty digesting the image of my seventeen-year-old friend sitting on this sixty-year-old man's lap. I was jolted out of my confusion when he started talking to me.

"I know someone you should meet, Celia," the older man said to me, Dana's arm around his neck.

"I have a boyfriend," I looked down at the table.

"Well, this guy has a lot of money to spend."

I nodded my head but didn't respond. The air in the room felt dense and the situation was closing in on me. I didn't know exactly how to label what was happening, but I could feel in my gut that something big was wrong.

"What's your favorite car?" the older man started again, staring at me.

I looked up for a moment at him, but the sight of him with Dana made my stomach turn.

"This guy's got a black Trans Am. It's really cool. He has lots of money he could spend on you."

Though something impending felt bad and wrong, he'd piqued my interest. I had never known anyone that "had a lot of money," and my relatively innocent mind merely envisioned having a boyfriend with money, meaning we could go out on real dates to restaurants and the movies—things I'd never done before. Maybe I could even introduce a guy like that to my parents and have them be proud that I found someone successful. The proposition made me curious and I asked about him, surprising myself.

"He's tall," Dana said from the man's lap. She'd met him before.

"Red hair. Older, though." I stopped on her face when she said this.

I didn't have time to ask Dana to define "older" before the man told me that he had a bedroom in case I wanted to get to know his friend. He told me that I was really going to like him. But the mention of the bedroom and the man being "older" pulled me right out of my naïve fantasy. Scared, I was still a virgin, and today was not the day I was going to lose that, especially in this situation.

"No, thanks. I don't think I want to meet him," I told them cordially and puffed my cigarette. Jessie and Dana began pressuring me to go on, to give the man a try.

Pushing Dana off his lap, the older man walked to the phone and picked up the receiver. "I can call him right now?" he motioned toward me. "He'd love you. You're just his type," the older man pressured.

"No, I'm not into red heads," I told them with a cavalier smoke, feigning coolness. I didn't want them to see me uneasy or afraid. "I've got to go now anyway," I told them and stretched up out of my chair. Trying to stop me, Dana asked me to wait for her, saying she was worried I'd get lost on my way back to school. I assured her that I wouldn't and left.

For days after that encounter, Dana asked me to go back over to the man's house. "We could party. You know he'll have beer and cigarettes there. I could get him to buy some weed for us, too." The harder she pushed, the more reluctant I became.

I grew distant from Dana and Jessie. If I saw one of them walking down the street, I'd dip into an alley to avoid them. When one of them came to my house, I told my mother to say I wasn't home. I didn't realize at the time that they were interacting with a trafficker and I was supposed to be his next victim. I just got the sense that they were people I should avoid.

Shortly after my visit with them to the older man's house, Dana and Jessie started running away from home, or at least that's what we heard. We noticed the police being called to their house on occasion—domestic disputes—and over time, the family moved away. I never knew what really became of any of them for a time.

Dana kept in occasional touch with me. She would call my mom's house and ask for me, but I couldn't shake that uneasy feeling about her. I continued to avoid her. Even though I hadn't understood what was going on that day, I had a funny feeling that something wasn't right—something dangerous. When I did finally accept her call one day, she asked me for money. She was in some form of trouble, or she was addicted to drugs, and something was wrong. I couldn't decipher her story. I told her that I didn't have any money, and once I hung up, I told my mother to always say I wasn't home if she called again.

At nineteen, I moved into my own apartment, and without any real future trajectory, I had a lot of parties to occupy my time. I corralled my friends to drink and do whatever drugs we could afford. It was the early eighties, and our extra money bought hits of acid or double dome THC, which came in pill form. Most of the time, though, when we didn't have extra cash, we stuck to drinking beer and smoking weed. Occasionally, a party would get out of hand—someone would reveal a gun stashed in their waistband or a new girl would get too drunk—and I'd have to fetch Camille from her house across the street to help me kick everyone out. New people were always trouble, but I knew how to handle my core group of friends.

Most of the time, I knew everyone at my parties. They were all from my block, or they were from the East side, where my boyfriend, Jake, was from. Jake had been stabbed through the neck years back and had major reconstructive surgery, making him more skittish than most, and justifiably so, but one night, his heightened anxiety caught my attention. A new crew of three men I'd never seen before showed up with one of Jake's friends, making themselves at home. My apartment was small and I could see everyone in every room from the living room. From the back of the room, I noticed one of the strange men quietly getting agitated. I could hear him quelling about how tough he was, about things he'd done, trying to prove some unprovoked dominance in the room. As he raised his arms in gesture, I noticed a gun tucked into his pants, and when I looked at Jake, the fear on his face triggered me to take action.

I slipped out of the apartment through the bedroom and ran to Camille's house, telling her the situation. Camille, without hesitation, stormed across the street, and threw the door opened. Stunned, everyone watched as she walked to the stereo and cut the music, yelling, "Everyone get the fuck out!" They all listened. But many nights required vigilance and temperament to keep things under control. We partied with abandon and were warped from drugs and alcohol most of the time. My apartment became a hub for this sort of activity, making it both a fun and dangerous place to be. To me, though, it was home, on my block, in my neighborhood, with my people.

A year later, I got a phone call from Dana asking to see me. I was shocked to hear from her, but soon after I agreed, she pulled up in front of my house. She wasn't alone, though. An African-American man was driving her. His hair was permed and he was dressed nicely, if not over the top. He adorned a pinky ring that looked more expensive than anything I had ever seen, and he had a strong, clean scent about him that I could smell from the stoop. He looked like a pimp, and he didn't get out of the car.

Dana walked up to my stoop, asking if she could borrow some money. She needed a hundred dollars. She said she was getting her life together and that she was trying to raise money for a deposit on an apartment. She was a wreck, and I thought back to our last experience together. I hadn't realized it then, what was happening in that house, on that day. I didn't have the right knowledge or language to know that they were trying to recruit me—I only knew the situation felt wrong and dangerous. I didn't put it together at the time that they were trying to encourage me to sell sex to my first customer. I didn't understand until this moment that I had come so close to becoming a trafficking victim, and here was Dana, a victim herself, the fallout shakily standing in front of me.

If I'd had a hundred dollars, which I didn't, I surely wasn't going to hand it to her to give to her pimp. When she read my reticence, Dana explained that she was in trouble and that her friend in the car would be extremely upset if I didn't give her some money. She pleaded with me, her eyes big and drooping with despair, tired. I felt sorry for her, and I gave her the only twenty bucks I had. Dana thanked me and left.

Months later, Dana called again and confirmed that the man in the car had been a pimp, but that she had escaped to Illinois to start a new life. Again, she asked me to send her some money, to which I declined and hung up the phone. I didn't take any more calls from Dana, and while I felt sympathy for her, I was nervous to try and help her at all.

I was growing into my twenties, into real adulthood, and the sense of power and confidence that I once adorned around my shoulders was slowly being sloughed off and replaced with insecurity and doubt. I fell into dysfunctional and violent relationship after dysfunctional and violent relationship. The easy fade of popularity, the meaninglessness of it all, began to sink in and I realized that I had nothing, not even a real sense of self-worth. I hadn't any accomplishments to be proud of. I wasn't making any real money, and when I wasn't high or drunk, the reality of it all set in in such a concrete way that it made my head and my heart thump with anxiety again. I felt reduced into my former self all over again—small, scared, unsure. The world continued to prove that it had little to offer but fear and danger as the people I knew crumbled around me.

Over my lifetime to that point, my mother snatched away any pride I held for too long. Her timely comments hacked away at my self-esteem, and her and my father's habitual neglect left me feeling lonely at the core. Even once I was on my own, the damage had been cut so deep that it'd become a disability, crippling me when I was sober. I spent so much time trying to show people that I was alright, that I was unbreakable, I forgot to care for myself. I didn't know how to build a real life—how to not just survive, but to thrive, because surely this wasn't it.

Looking around after speaking to Dana, my eyes opened to a new reality surrounding me. I could see what I hadn't been able to see before: that sex trafficking had infiltrated my neighborhood, that it had profoundly affected my friends, that it was occurring on my block this whole time, and I came to see that several of my friends had been trafficked within a two-block radius. I thought about Emma Kay. My heart hurt for her. It was so close to me, tearing apart the people and the families around me, but it was so hard to identify underneath all of the revolving abuse and trauma we'd all endured growing up. It was this insidious thing, eating up the young girls around us, enticing them into a world they didn't know could kill them, and I had been blind to it up until that point.

I came to surmise that the father I resented was probably the reason traffickers avoided me. In their lurking, they likely targeted girls with less forceful fathers—girls more vulnerable than me—and I'm grateful for that because I believe his mere presence saved me. While I hated my relationship with my father—the way he ignored me, his distaste for our family, how disloyal he was—it was his crass and heated nature that likely scared off predators from me and my sisters. So, fortunately, no, I have never been a trafficking victim, but I knew then that I might be able save those who were.

CHAPTER EIGHT

The Long Road

When my father announced that I would be going to college, I was shocked. I barely graduated high school, and I graduated high school late because I failed a history course during my junior year that I had to repeat during the summer of senior year. I should have been the last person that my father agreed to pay for college courses for. I'm not sure if he saw something in me that I just couldn't see anymore, but the thought of me being book smart had vacated my mind a long time before that, replaced with drinking beer and smoking weed. Maybe my parents just panicked, thinking that their last child wasn't going to make it in the world if they didn't do something drastic.

All of my sisters were out of the house, working, doing well. My parents bribed me to go to college by giving me one of their apartments to live in and a small checking account with which to buy books. I happily started school. Not because I was in pursuit of the great education

I would be getting, but because I had an apartment to party in and a checking account I could use to buy beer. My father must have assumed I became really studious because I was cashing checks every week, supposedly buying books and materials from the university bookstore for classes. I took advantage of the fact that my father never went to college to tell him that needing materials for school was an ongoing process as a student.

Even though I had a keen ability to understand and grasp concepts quickly, I hadn't spent enough time in school to learn how to write well. I wasn't confident enough to go to the University of Toledo's main campus. Instead, I signed up to attend the University of Toledo Community and Technical College. The first course I took was a basic writing course. The requirement was to write ten well-formed paragraphs to pass the course. I promptly failed. I felt defeated. I hadn't learned to write a simple paragraph. Not being able to do this gnawed at me. I was depressed. I was angry. I got high. But it was still there.

There is one trait that a Williamson has. If you tell us not to do something, we will likely do it. We don't like to be defeated, and my motivation for bettering my life was still twisted—I knew if I failed school that the money for parties would stop. I retook the course, determined, and tried my best. I failed again. I couldn't move forward without this course. I took it a third time, finally passing the basic writing course.

It took me four years to get a two-year community and technical degree in social services. When I moved from the community and technical college over to the main campus of the University of Toledo, the schools hadn't communicated with each other, and many of the social work courses I took at the community and technical college didn't count toward the four-year accredited bachelor's degree. Anger and frustration don't properly describe how upset I was. To struggle to get to this point only to find out that, essentially, I had to start over if I wanted a bachelor's degree was disheartening. I felt like all was lost. I believed I had wasted my father's money. I was homicidal. I was suicidal. I tell people today when there are setbacks to go home, feel homicidal, feel suicidal, and then meet your barrier head on. With that spirit about me, I spent another five years getting the four-year degree in social work.

My social work degree helped me to put my family, my friends, and my neighborhood into perspective, and I was grateful for my education. I was able to see both the benefits of the people in my life and the work that needed to be done in my community. What I came to understand was that my mother and my father, who I sometimes hated as a teenager, stood between me and the harsh realities of my neighborhood. I'm convinced my father's strong presence in my neighborhood helped me avoid many of the problems I could have faced. Because I feared him, I stayed in school. Because the neighborhood feared him, I avoided a lot of the fights other kids had. I didn't have to fight for my ranking and position in the neighborhood—my father owned most of the houses on the block and simply would have evicted any tenant and their children that would have challenged his daughter.

As a child and adolescent, I couldn't appreciate the cruel harshness of my mother's parenting style. Now, her parenting style makes sense and fits into the ecosystem of the callous environment I lived in. She wasn't perfect, but poor people in low-income urban environments like mine usually have a more punitive parenting style. Not because parents of poor children are bad people, but because their first priority is to keep their children as safe and prepared for the harsh realities of life as possible. As antithetical as that sounds, these parents know that they can't be everywhere, and that there will be times when their children will have to think for themselves and make decisions that could alter their lives. So kids have to learn to navigate dangerous terrain. They have to learn to properly assess risks and make safe decisions. They have to learn to rely on their gut, and when they have a feeling something isn't right, they need to remove themselves from the situation or find ways to handle themselves in risky situations. I learned to do this over and over growing up. From the near sexual assaults to the seat at a trafficker's table with my friends, Dana and Jessie. My parents, in their harsh parenting style, taught me to rely on myself and to use my intuition.

I even better understood my parents' marriage and am no longer so quick to pass judgement. Marriages are difficult. They are complex. No one understands the intricacies of a relationship more than the two people inside it. I decided to show my parents some grace and allow them to judge the relationship they were in without my interference. I came to realize I was part of one of the few families in the neighborhood that had a father who worked and a mother who took care of the home. I had hot meals, clothes, shoes, heat, lights, and guidance. They loved me and did their best with what they had, financially and emotionally.

Over the years, the neighborhood women sitting at my mother's table, telling their stories of risk, violence, and danger, taught me everything I needed to know about how to be a woman and to be safe. When safety is at risk, safety becomes the most important lesson to learn. At first, I thought to be able to sit at my mother's table you had to have experienced violence. In my twisted logic, I thought that sitting there, smoking a cigarette, drinking coffee, and telling a war story of survival was a rite of passage.

Every time a woman arrived at my mother's kitchen table, we had to get up and give them our seat. We hadn't earned that seat yet. You had to earn your seat at this table, and you did that by experiencing all the trappings of adulthood, including surviving violence. I thought being a woman meant you took care of everyone and everything, and that you knew how to navigate the potential for sexual or physical abuse. Violence was inevitable. I remember my niece sitting at my mother's table with stitches in her head from her boyfriend, and my cousin, who had been kidnapped, raped, and held for days by her boyfriend, at my mother's table. I remember hearing our tenants' stories and my mother periodically calling the police to get a tenant's man to stop beating her. These occurrences were normal in my neighborhood. My young mind thought they were expected. In fact, I would go on to become involved as a victim of domestic violence across two relationships myself.

I spent over five years in a relationship with an abusive man—a man who didn't respect me, who was an alcoholic and a crack addict—and after five years with him, to my surprise, I found myself pregnant. I was elated, but I knew I needed to be a single mother. I finished my degree and graduated in my cap and gown while pregnant. Afterwards, I kicked out my boyfriend. Not backing down, the very next time he was drunk and mad and was trying to kick my front door in, I called the police and they took him to jail. He spent weeks stalking me, calling me, and showing up at my door, threatening me. I was extremely scared, but I kept myself determined to get rid of him. I filed for child support and pressed charges against him, all for the sake of my daughter.

Now that I'm older, I understand that violence isn't inevitable. Men don't come pre-packaged as abusers. Men are products of their experiences just like women are. Through their stories, the women at the table taught me to identify danger, to understand risk, and to try to avoid violence. Those were powerful lessons that I carried with me. I understand that's why I would come to be able to do anti-trafficking work. I knew violence existed. I knew women and girls were sometimes the victims of horrific physical and sexual violence. I had my own experiences with both. I kept their examples in my head and in my heart as I faced the work I would do for the next twenty-five years.

Some of my female friends were lucky enough to tuck themselves away in very safe marriages. They were able to move out of the neighborhood and raise children and grandchildren. For some kids, learning to avoid physical danger, but also navigate, accept, and expect that life will be difficult and that opportunities will be scarce is a harsh lesson, but one that is taught early on--and one that is played out in our social circles. For instance, people in poor neighborhoods joke more with each other, they tease more severely, preparing you to withstand the pressures that racism, sexism, and classism will provide you in the real world. Because of this early preparation, I believe poor kids are more prepared for rejection than any other kids, because they are taught to succeed despite what happens, not as a reaction to what is offered.

It is assumed you should work twice as hard to get half as much. We expect to wait in long lines, for things to not work out the first time, and to be turned down. But much like I did, some youth become angry, slip into drug and alcohol use, and give up. Some ambitious youth gravitate towards the jobs that are available in these neighborhoods, namely drugs, gang membership, gun sales, and selling others through sex trafficking. A balance is needed between preparing youth to face the harsh realities of life as a poor kid, and demonstrating enough love, support, and care that they will continue to try. I was lucky in that I had parents that pushed me and wanted something better for my life. Many youth in these communities face many risk factors, but very few protective factors that serve to insulate them from abuse, support them and meet their needs, and encourage them to want something better for their lives.

Youth in low-income neighborhoods know that if they don't pay attention to or follow the rules in the real world, they will face harsher consequences than other kids. They have to be supported, and taught to channel their anger into trying again or pursuing another path and to not to give up. When I became angry at a world that denied me, my gun was the most powerful thing that I owned. I confused that type of power with my inability to access real power in the world. But having a family and learning important lessons from the women at my mother's table helped me put the gun down that night. Although I couldn't see it then, not everyone has the support I had, and some experiences alter the lives of youth forever. I felt both lucky and blessed to be in my family, on my block, and to have been raised in my neighborhood.

Parenting in this harsher style keeps children in line, because young men of color who don't obey the rules are incarcerated at more than five times the rate of whites, charged at higher rates, convicted at higher rates, and receive longer sentences in jails and prisons. Girls who don't pay attention, who aren't hypervigilant, may be assaulted or taken advantage of as sex trafficking victims. Several studies report that poor girls and girls of color experience significantly higher rates of sexual abuse as children and sexual assault as women. Girls learn to be hypervigilant about their surroundings, who they are with, and the intentions of the people they are with. Parents who don't actively teach these survival skills leave their daughters vulnerable to fend for themselves against a society that provides less protection to poor girls.

It's strange because, at the same time, poor neighborhoods are one of the most loving and accepting places on the planet. I feel most comfortable in poor neighborhoods, including mine. Anyone can be accepted there. I felt loved unconditionally in my neighborhood because of who I was and not because of what I did or what I owned. I laughed harder in my hood than anywhere else. People from my neighborhood speak with their heart. They are authentic. They aren't pretentious, and once accepted, you know you are welcome to whatever they have to share. I have not found that anywhere else. The food is the best, the company is both warm and entertaining, and the hospitality is genuine. I realized that my life in the north end of Toledo was one of the best educations I could have received to prepare me for the work I was meant to do.

Approximately one-third of women worldwide, that's almost one billion, will suffer intimate partner violence or non-partner sexual violence in their lifetime. But the violence women and girls suffer is proportionate to their protections in society. Class, race, and gender help determine the level and type of violence, with poor, disenfranchised girls suffering the most violent and pervasive abuse. In addition to the sexual harassment, stalking, and other forms of intimidation girls suffer, some of the most insidious violence that is perpetrated against girls is not physical or sexual. It's emotional. It's verbal.

Girls suffer psychological abuse perpetrated by a society that, in many ways, tells them their value to our society is in their physical beauty, which is defined by men. If we are not a size two, aged twenty-two, and white with blonde hair, we aren't measuring up in the U.S., which holds age, race, and size as considerable symbols of beauty. Even though women represent 50.8% of the population and control 80% of consumer spending, they are only 3% of the creative directors in advertising. Their image is still overwhelmingly controlled by men who prefer to perpetuate these myths and maintain the status quo. It is a human rights violation and should never be tolerated, excused, or accepted. Yet, in some respects, these double standards are accepted as a part of life for women.

All of this combined subjugates and subordinates women to a status of second class citizenship. Of course, in the work I would go on to do, I had no time to debate the image of women and their relationship to violence in society. These intellectual conversations were left in the classroom. I had fundamental work to be done where violence through commercial sexual exploitation was real, it happened daily, and no one was doing anything about it.

Childhood home

Mother's table

Celia's parents

Celia (center) and Emma Kay (right)

Celia, third grade

Celia and friends

On the porch

PART II

My father never really talked to me. When I got my degree, he would talk at me, maybe once a year. The one thing he did tell me after I got my degree was that it's the tree that bends that thrives. I had no idea what that meant, and passed it off as the ravings of a dictator. But now that I'm older, I think I understand. The wind is much stronger than the tree. It has the ability to destroy entire buildings. Wind can stir up the water and cause great floods. It can put a fire out or it can agitate the fire even more. And the real old African saying is, "The wind does not break the tree that bends." In my work with women and youth involved in prostitution and sex trafficking, I needed to bend. I needed to ignore the formal policies, procedures, and accepted social rules about professionalism. I needed to remove the fear and the distance we keep between those we perceive as different from us. Before I could help, I needed to meet women and youth where they were, in their space, at their time, and on their terms. I needed to be the tree that bends.

CHAPTER NINE

An Introduction to the Streets

My daughter, Lisa, was born on December 3rd, 1988. I was living in a house that I rented from my parents for fifty dollars a month. The roof leaked, so I bought pans from Goodwill to catch the water. I had mice and roaches, but it was shelter for us. I encouraged the drinkers in the neighborhood to drink and hang out in front of my house because that at least provided me a level of defense for me and my daughter. I could deal with a broken down house as long as we were safe inside of it.

My north end neighborhood, in all, spanned fifty blocks, and I found a job as a social worker just a few blocks down from where I lived. Being a social worker on the north end of Toledo empowered me in a lot of ways, but mostly, I learned a great deal about the people I'd grown up with. I learned so many things that I didn't know but only felt, and this knowledge let me piece it all together—helped build a full understanding of my world, making my work incredibly effective.

Most people in my neighborhood could only read at an eighth grade level, and the urban Appalachian families in my neighborhood had been there over generations. I knew about them, having lived in their culture for twenty-five years, having friends from their households, like Emma Kay and Mary. I knew that they were proud, hard-working people with free spirits. But I learned that more Appalachian people sign up for the military than any other group—that they are traditionally both poor and patriotic, and while that might seem like a queer mixture of misconception, many Appalachian families have ancestral roots that stem from Tennessee, Kentucky, West Virginia, and other states that weave through the Appalachian Mountains. They come from families that built these states, homesteading and raising families on the land, working in factories and retiring with a monetary cushion that could sustain future generations. The Appalachian people's pride and patriotism lay in their contribution to the building and expansion of America, their sense of stability and unique talents.

Originally, the Appalachian people settled in the hills and hollows of Appalachian states because they had a fierce sense of independence and wanted to live by their own rules in sovereign communities. They grew their own crops and raised their own animals for sustenance. When mining companies and lumber companies moved into these areas to create industry, they raped the land of its lumber and displaced many Appalachian people. Other companies took the coal and minerals from the land, and they employed the Appalachian people from these communities in their companies. Because the land had been claimed by industry and the people were forced to work in the mills and factories for money, the companies opened stores where workers could purchase food and other items of necessity, extending credit to the people who owed most of their paychecks back to the company store.

When the companies realized that mineral rights to the land the Appalachian people lived on were worth a fortune, they asked the people to sign lengthy documents prepared by lawyers. When they refused, the companies hired expensive law firms and acquired rights to the minerals on Appalachian land through the courts. They ran sludge and chemicals over the land, poisoning any potential for crop growth. After it all, new industry had completely taken over, getting rich on Appalachian land and resources, leaving the Appalachian people disparaged.

In the sixties and seventies, many Appalachian families migrated to Pennsylvania and Ohio to find factory work. Being victims of abuse and exploitation, Appalachian families typically distrust people in suits, long and lengthy forms, or official documents. They prefer personal relationships and face-to-face communication. They settled in easily, buying homes and raising families, but the economic crash and resulting financial devastation that swept the country in the late seventies and early eighties hit Appalachian families who were living far from the mountains hard. With the closing of the factories, Appalachian families were forced to take government assistance to pay their rent and buy food for their families. Quickly, these families were assimilated into marginalized communities like mine.

In the eighties, low-income housing was built to accommodate the effects of the economic downturn. As the hierarchy of the American class system broke down, the systematic racism built into it left many

African-Americans on the front lines of poverty, placing them high on the low-income housing lists. As housing was built in the north end and converted, African-Americans flooded these neighborhoods to occupy housing, as did Appalachian families. This created racial tension, fights, and separation. But poverty has a way of evening the playing field, because when you're all in need, it's hard to hold onto racist beliefs. At some point, you have to borrow sugar or corn or meat from one another. There is a necessary reliance on your neighbor that middle class people don't need to have. At some point, you all just become humans living together in the projects--in old, dilapidated houses, built in centuries past.

But Appalachian families brought their traditions with them. In rural Appalachia, it was acceptable to allow your children to explore their environment and to learn who they were in the process. In transplanting those skills to the urban north end of Toledo, Appalachian youth who explored their environment became vulnerable to drugs, crime, trafficking and exploitation, including Emma Kay.

The next time I saw Emma Kay was on Lagrange Street during the summer, shortly before I started my anti-trafficking work. She was walking down the street, but she was in the street. She was visibly looking at cars and yelling out to the drivers as they drove by. I thought to myself, "Look at this crazy girl." I didn't recognize her. Driving by, I got close enough to see her face and for her to recognize me. The moment seared as I saw the shell of my friend, Emma Kay.

Emma abruptly turned away from me and walked onto the sidewalk, headed toward a bar. I waved at her, slowed down, and rolled down the window. I yelled her name, but she ignored me and disappeared into the bar. I thought that was so strange. I couldn't imagine why she would ignore me, particularly because she had been so focused on the cars driving by. I wanted to chat with her, catch up with her—just have some sort of interaction—and I was confused when she didn't want to talk to me. There was nothing to do, though, and I wasn't sure what to think, so I just drove off, soon forgetting about the encounter.

At twenty-eight years old, with a bachelor's degree in social work, I started working in a community center that served children and families. The center had been a staple of the neighborhood for over a hundred years, and I was very proud to be a part of it. In the twenties, the center, then coined "The Friendly Center,"—"friendly" to all who entered and "center" of the community—started as a home for women. Over time, the center developed settlement houses to help the poor, and assisted children, youth, families, and seniors. In its hay day, when I was there, the center offered psychosocial groups for women and youth, recreational activities, events, food, case management, home visits, and more.

Out of two buildings, I worked in an old two-story historic brick house that had been refurbished to include a large dining room where we fed seniors every day, a few meeting rooms in the back, a large living room equipped with sparse furnishings, and a set of offices for staff to work with families, where we provided them with support and groups, case management, summer day camp programming, and one-on-one help. My mother and my neighborhood friend, Vidette, both worked in the kitchen to prepare meals for the kids in the neighborhood.

Being from the neighborhood we served, our agency was culturally sensitive. We understood the oppressive history of both African-Americans and Appalachian whites. We respected both cultures, we'd broken bread with them, and we had to build trusting relationships with our neighbors. The people we served preferred building trust over time, face-to-face, and we had a saying at our center: "You haven't started the work until you're at the kitchen table." A seat at this table meant that meaningful work could begin.

Phone calls and visits on residents' porches were only preliminary, polite gestures. Talking to people through the crack of their door is only the beginning. We waited to be invited in, to sit with them at their table—we built genuine, caring relationships that helped changed lives, in the hopes of empowering our community.

As an employee for the community center, one of my duties was to run weekly empowerment and prevention groups with African-American and Appalachian mothers in the neighborhood, as well as groups with at-risk teens. I also helped families acquire needed resources, and provided work opportunities for those court-ordered offenders who were serving restitution at our center. I helped people apply for social security benefits, facilitated groups for troubled youth, worked in the summer day camp each year, and conducted home visits to do assessments and offer interventions for families. Those who couldn't read would bring their mail to the center for me to read. I helped clients advocate for themselves and their families when engaged with child protection, the welfare department, or the housing authority. We gave out food on a weekly basis. I did conflict management between teenagers and their parents. I participated in community-based meetings to collaborate with other agencies for the benefit of the neighborhood and clients. When there was a new program or new policy, we went door-to-door to hand out materials and educate our neighbors about how the new changes would affect them. We did it all.

After a long day of community outreach, I stopped at the local grocery store to pick up a few items on my way home. Shortly into my shopping, the quality of the food upset me. The vegetables were not fresh, the meat looked less-than-desirable, there was an odor pouring from unkept coolers, and the floors were visibly dirty. Up to that point, I'd been blind to the difference between this store and the grocery stores outside of our neighborhood.

Frustrated, I ventured outside of the north end to other grocery stores that served middle class neighborhoods, cost-comparing and checking prices of suburban stores against our own. Realizing the stark difference, I went door-to-door in my neighborhood with a flyer to alert the residents that if they contacted me, I would pick them up once a month, after food stamps were issued, and take them out to a suburban grocery store where the prices were cheaper and the food was fresh.

Eventually, the executive director of the community center, David J. Morris, received a call from the local grocery store, complaining that I was driving away business. David supported my conquest and let the store owner know that he needed to change his practices, validating my work and advocacy. The Friendly Center was supported by the United Way, and was a place where the disenfranchised could go to be heard and empowered. My actions embodied our mission, and I felt supported and safe there.

I often went into sections of the projects that were ruled by gangs and drug dealers to pick up children for tutoring because I had worked with their mothers or siblings, and because everyone knew my intentions in these parts of town. I always felt safe, even protected. I knew the projects. I knew the streets. I knew who had power in various regions across neighborhoods and who to talk to. We worked through mutual respect, and I climbed the established hierarchies to create needed change from within. I had been groomed for this work through a childhood wrought with poverty and lessons learned on the same streets.

I knew all of the programs and resources in town. I knew who to call and who not to call. I knew who was eligible for what, how long it might take to get a resource, and how to circumvent the system if I could. I knew all of the hustlers and their hustles. I knew that neighbors stopped paying their gas bill in September or October only so they could get the shut off notice in November and become eligible for a social service program to pay the bill so they could use their money to buy Christmas gifts in December. I directed them on where to get a Thanksgiving turkey and the sides so that each family could have a hearty Thanksgiving meal.

I knew that food stamps were seven on the ten, meaning if you sold your food stamps, for every ten dollars that you sold, you could get seven dollars in cash. I knew that if someone sold them for five on the ten, they were desperate, and I needed to contact them and find out what might be going on. I would let the seniors come to our free clothing store. I knew they were taking clothes in all types of styles and sizes because they would sell them at yard sales, using the money to help pay for some of their prescriptions. I knew the streets, and I loved working there. This was my home, my block, my neighborhood, my people.

CHAPTER TEN
Revelation

I passed women working on the street on my way to work every day. They sauntered around street corners, waiting to be hailed by men in cars. This was part of the street that I didn't know as well, and my unfamiliarity stemmed from an unspoken resentment. To be honest, at first, I didn't like these women. I wanted them to go away, to disappear, so that our children and families wouldn't be exposed to the sex trade happening on our streets or to the drugs they brought into our community. There were others that shared my disdain, but they threw water and pop bottles at the women as they passed by. A secret part of me resented those women for the work they did, but I disliked the people that threw water on them more.

Working the streets and living in the same neighborhood I served did, however, create an economic disparity for me. I was still a part of the cycle of it all. Even with my bachelor's degree, as a social worker, I was making $18,000 a year with a baby to support. I was living in an old, run down house that my parents owned. They let me live there for fifty dollars a month and, most times, I couldn't afford to pay that. The duplex directly across the street from my house was empty, as was the house next door. Both of these had been empty for years. On the other side of my house was an open field. I had mice and occasionally roaches. My one-story house, built in the early 1900s, leaked in eight places. I bought pots from Goodwill and used them to catch the rain. I carpeted the house by taking carpeting out of a dumpster that had been thrown out by a business. My furniture was given to me by my parents, and it was from previous tenants who had left it behind. I had a bed, but preferred to sleep on a mattress I'd put on the floor in the dining room because that's where the heater was and that's where I could keep myself and my baby warm. Plus, the dining room was the center of the house and allowed me to hear if anyone was breaking in. It was now the nineties, and drugs and violence were rampant as the crack era was in full swing in my community.

I didn't have a phone to call the police in an emergency, but I had a gun. My mother lived two doors down, so I could run there if I could make it. My daughter and I mostly ate what my mother cooked. Living this way made me an empathetic social worker—I could relate to the people I served. We were one and the same. I needed welfare assistance for a few years, including food stamps, and I took advantage of the Women, Infants, and Children program (WIC). WIC provided me and my daughter with the nutrition we needed to stay healthy.

Accepting welfare was a humiliating experience for me. Not so much because of the thought of accepting it, but it was because of the treatment I received from the workers. I ended up paying for my daughter's birth myself. She was ten years old when I paid it off. She was also ten years old before she was covered under a health insurance plan.

I often thought about how I'd become the woman I was. There were so many times in my life when I veered left when I should have gone right, so many times where my thinking and my behavior seemed unmanageable, erratic—so many times I had made mistakes that could've ruined my life forever. But here I was, no matter how difficult the struggle may be, I had my own office and a college degree, and that's when it hit me.

The women selling themselves on the street came into my thoughts abruptly, and a cluster of profound questions planted themselves in my brain: *Why do you hate these women out on the street? In hating them, are you living up to your Christian principles? There was a time in your life when people passed judgment and stigmatized you. Are you focusing your primary purpose as a social worker, which is to work with the poor, vulnerable and oppressed, on everyone who needs you? Or have you been working with the worthy, deserving and beautiful, patting yourself on the back for a job well done? Are you really a feminist or just a social justice advocate that talks a good game? And most importantly, how close have you come to being just like them?*

There was an evolution happening inside of me, and I knew I had to deal with my resentments—get to the source of them so that I could fulfill my own code of ethics. These women deserved as much as I had to offer. They were in need, too. I had an epiphany at my desk that day and thought about these things long and hard before I was able to shake it all off. I would build upon these thoughts later with a more open mind and heart.

My superiors at The Friendly Center, David Morris and James Colbert, were constant supporting mentors to me. They were my yin and my yang. I didn't understand their value until much later. These men taught me the best in social work, but they also taught me how to understand men, relate to men, and love men. I needed them both for my personal and professional development.

David was an executive director in every sense of the word. He worked day and night to keep the center open. He wrote grants, went to meetings, gave speeches in churches, developed strategic plans, and managed funds. David was a tall, middle-aged white man who was a pastor previously from the South. He was adorned with a full head of black wavy hair, a moustache, and wore a suit to work every day. At the Friendly Center, he motivated people to give and told them why it was right to give and keep the center open. He was inspirational. He loved the neighborhood and what the center stood for. He could be harsh in that he didn't have the time nor the inclination to soft step in areas that he was passionate about. He was not one to provide soft appeasement, and he didn't have much patience, so David wasn't tasked with engaging clients, but was effectual in many other crucial ways. I understood him. I respected him. He was there to keep the doors of the center open, and I learned so much from him.

James was the complete opposite of David. James was a large, husky black man that was as kind and cuddly as they come. He had a big smile and a hug for everyone. James loved weed and was a product of sixties social work—when they hired community organizers that hung out, met neighbors, and helped organize the community. He worked with the kids at the center. When he organized with adults, he made them feel like they could be better people. He made me want to tap into my higher self, my better self. I followed James around as much as I could. If James stopped too fast, I would have run into the back of him.

Not only did these men mentor and support me, but much to my surprise one day, David repeated what my father did for me by telling me that it was time for me to get my master's degree. I had been thinking about it and kicking the idea around, but I favored the idea of talking about what I was going to do instead of actually doing it.

David and James believed in me. They believed in the work I did and what I was capable of. They saw me—they saw my potential in the way that I yearned for someone to see me when I was a little girl. They felt about me how I felt about myself, and I was honored to be gifted this opportunity. I'd always wanted more for my life, but I didn't know how to develop a plan or a pathway to improve my circumstances. I knew about school, I knew there was a path there where I could soar, but there was no point of entry for me available, so I'd let that dream go in service of what I already had. Secretly, deep down, I did want to pursue my master's degree, but I had no real plans to obtain it. There were far too many barriers to entry. And then David dropped the expectation right into my lap. He verbalized it and breathed it into the realm of possibility. Sometimes we lean into the dream that others have for us. No one rises to low expectations. David had high expectations for me, and I wanted to go along with him and bet on myself to succeed.

The first fear that crossed my mind, though, was that I wouldn't be accepted into any programs. Having barely earned a 2.6 GPA upon graduation with my bachelor's, I knew almost every master's program required at least a 2.7 GPA to even apply. I didn't want to disappoint David and his high expectations of me. I was inspired by his belief in me, and I envied who he was as a person.

While David was telling me that I was going to get a master's degree, James bought tickets for the whole team to go see Les Brown at the University of Toledo. I didn't want to go. I didn't understand what it was going to be about, and I just wanted to go home, my mind heavy with indecision. James playfully hit me on the back and said, "Come on. You're not doing nothing anyway." So, together, we drove to the University of Toledo and I sat down in Doerman Theatre, thinking it was a waste of my time.

Les Brown delivered a presentation that changed my life. He told me that I could do anything I wanted to do, and that I was only limited by myself, guided by my fears. He encouraged me to stop living in fear and to start living in my dreams. While I know there was an entire audience of people in the room that day, listening to the same thing I was listening to, Brown's message deeply resonated with me and was very powerful for me. I was really embarrassed to gush over the profound feeling I had, so I kept it to myself, but inside, I was bursting with new-found inspiration—inspiration that I desperately needed.

I was invigorated. It was a new day and I had a new plan for my life. Life wouldn't take me where it wanted anymore. I would take my life where I wanted it to go. That night, I applied for master's programs. I wasn't even eligible to apply, but as Les told me, I would allow other people to tell me no, but I would never tell myself no. I submitted applications to the best schools in the region, including the University of Michigan in Ann Arbor and Case Western Reserve in Cleveland. In the required personal statement, I sold myself the best I could. I said everything, from telling them that I would work hard to telling them that I was a poor black child that needed a chance. I said everything I thought might work in my favor, and all of it was true nonetheless.

Not only did I apply to master's programs, I promptly ended my abusive relationship with my daughter's father. This would be the second and last abusive relationship I would be in. Les' words danced around my mind: "Many people are afraid that they will die alone, and so they stay with someone not right for them. Here's my thought. I believe in a 'one to a box' theory, because you will die in a box by yourself." These words hit me in the gut. He countered all of the women at my mother's kitchen table and offered me the chance to get on a new path and live the life I wanted. He was right. I had more to offer the world, and I deserved better treatment. I didn't know exactly what I would do with my life, but I would go to school and end my relationship. I knew that much when I left the University of Toledo that day.

On my way to work the next day, I passed a woman with dark hair that caught my eye. She was white, her clothes were dirty and didn't quite fit her right, and it was difficult to discern her age because of an apparent history of drug use. She didn't look like the glamorous stereotype of the street prostitutes you see on television. No. She wore a pair of second-hand slacks and a loose T-shirt, and stumbled up and down the block, paying particular attention to the cars driving by in hopes that a man will want to purchase sex. I knew once she caught a glimpse of me and saw that I was a woman, she would look away, so I passed by her and quickly waved and smiled in the second she glanced at me. She turned away still, and continued her patrol. She stayed in my thoughts throughout the rest of my week.

CHAPTER ELEVEN

A Hard Sell

To my elation, I received a call from Case Western asking me to come in for an interview. I asked my mother to go with me for support, and we borrowed my sister's car—the only working car in the family that could actually make the trip to Cleveland. I didn't value time then as much as I do now. The importance of being on time is a middle class value that simply wasn't instilled in me. I didn't need it to navigate my everyday life, so we left too late. Once on the road and when I realized how late we might be for the meeting, I sped up. A lot.

At eighty miles an hour in a fifty-five, I flew past a police officer who radioed my position to another officer ahead of us. As we neared him, the officer was standing outside his car, pointed at me and aggressively motioned for me to pull over. Later, my mother would recount the story in her kitchen, saying that I "pulled over on a dime and got nine and a half cents change." I pulled over quickly, the officer gave me an eighty-dollar ticket and let me go. We arrived forty-five minutes late for my interview at Case Western.

I rushed into the university and then slowed my pace before walking into the professor's office. His desk faced the wall directly across from the door, and he had his chair turned with his back against the desk and a newspaper held up to his face.

"Excuse me. I'm here for an appointment. Celia Williamson. I'm sorry I'm late," I started.

The professor lowered his paper and took a moment before responding, "Yes, you are." He then lifted the paper back up in front of his face and continued reading.

I stood in the doorway, quietly, unsure what to do.

I know now that being late greatly hindered my chance with the university, but I was so disconnected from any culture of success or the values that middle class people adhere to. I could see in that moment that the professor considered my lateness as a reflection of my character and made a snap decision about me. In that moment, I told myself to walk away. You've blown it. It's over. Save whatever is left of your dignity and just walk away. The voice inside my head was loud and compelling, but my feet stood firm and planted.

I stood there, listening to my heart argue with my head. This is your opportunity. This is your shot. You can't just walk away! And as quickly as my heart pleaded, my head rebutted. There was a war waging inside of me, wrapped up in anxiety, and I didn't have an answer. I couldn't logically make a decision and I felt paralyzed. Something inside of me knew that I was standing on the cusp of a turning point, and in horror, I felt my feet start to push forward.

I lifted my finger and pulled the professor's newspaper down. "Excuse me, sir," I looked at him. "I would like just a minute of your time to tell you what I want to do with my life and why I want to go to Case." There was screaming inside of my head. I was panicked, but that fear melted before it crested my skin. I appeared as collected as possible, and I persisted. "You see, I'm going to do great things," I continued, "and I would just like Case Western's name attached to those things."

The professor looked down over me from atop his glasses, perched at the end of his nose. He was agitated with me, but I'd piqued his curiosity. "Yes?" he inquired.

"Sir, I want to be successful. I want to make my mother and my father proud. I want to change lives. I want to add value to the world," I shuffled over to one of the chairs in front of his desk. "Mind if I sit down?" I said as I took a seat. I pulled the chair closer to his desk and continued talking. I told him all that I did for children and families at The Friendly Center, where I'd come from, and that I had both the heart and the guts to be a master's level social worker. I told him that I was a victim of domestic violence, but that was about to change. I told him that if he let me into Case Western that I would get all A's and B's, that he'd never have to worry about regretting this decision. I would be a wise choice.

After an hour of conversation with a man who held his emotions like a poker player with a winning hand, the professor told me that he had one condition upon which he would admit me to Case Western's program, and I told him that whatever it was, I would meet his expectation.

"I will personally walk your file over to admissions, but I want to be there when you graduate. I want to physically see you graduate," the professor peered at me with a serious look, and I knew I'd won my chance.

"Absolutely! Thank you, thank you, thank you," I hugged a man that didn't seem like the huggable type and continued to ramble with excitement and gratitude.

"Okay, okay," the professor pushed me off and looked sideways at me, silently affirming that he had high hopes for me.

I ran out to the car and excitedly told my mother the whole story. I told it to her over and over again, analyzing each part of the story, for the entire drive home. We celebrated in the car, and I knew right then that I was on my way. There were bigger things in store for me, and for once, those bigger things felt within my reach. My mother told me that she was proud of me because I showed courage. She said courage is being afraid and moving forward anyway. She told me that I showed courage enough to care about my future, and with this, I felt my world expand. Someone had given me a chance and I wouldn't waste it. I felt hope. Hope is a powerful emotion. I was ready to explore all the master's degree had to offer; ready to do real work and inspire real change. I had it all in me, and now others were seeing it, too.

On Monday morning, I was excited on my work way to work, ready to break the great news to David and James, but I hadn't forgotten about the dark-haired woman who had been lingering on the corner. I passed her again and waved at the most opportune moment. Again, she quickly looked away, but I drove by slowly. I wanted her to see me more clearly, and when she turned for the second time, I made sure she got a full view of my face and said, "Hi," through the passenger window. The woman looked back at me, took a puff of her cigarette, and then smashed it beneath her foot before turning and walking away. We went on like this for weeks.

The more I tried to interact with this woman and gain her trust, the more I thought about Emma Kay. I saw Emma in her, and I needed to know what had happened to her. Reflecting on my brief encounter with her, I came to understand that Emma Kay was engaged in street prostitution, and she must have felt a great deal of shame when I recognized her. She wasn't able to talk to me then. The only thing she could do was walk away and avoid the shame of looking at someone who held her past in their heart—someone who knew who Emma Kay really wanted to become.

I learned through her brother, Keith, that Emma Kay had an older sugar daddy. Sugar daddies are "tricks," or repeat customers with an emotional attachment to a sex worker, and they keep spending their money on the women they are infatuated with. Keith and others in his family tried their best to help Emma escape this life. When Emma's brother asked her not to leave with this person, Emma became extremely aggressive. The need for drugs was way too powerful and Emma couldn't hear Keith's pleas to save her life. The family lost touch with Emma for weeks at a time. They held their breath every time the news reported a body found, hoping and praying it wasn't Emma.

CHAPTER TWELVE

Tapped In

I might have been accepted into a master's program, and my position in life seemed to be elevating quickly, but I still had my ear and my heart close to the beat of the streets of my neighborhood. I was determined to use this new college opportunity to further my work, to give me more open access to the people in charge, to create change that would morph the way the next generation in my neighborhood would grow—the way my daughter and her daughters might see the world. To do that, I couldn't lose sight of where I came from and I had to stay deeply immersed in it all.

There is a certain psychology to the streets of any neighborhood, and I was never afraid to do street outreach because I knew how to navigate the terrain. I was wise with street smarts and I was in tune with the beat of the block. Working the street is like playing a violin. At first, it's awkward. You don't belong together and your body isn't comfortable with the way the violin rests under your chin, the way the bridge crests in front of your eyes, the way the strings cut along your fingertips. You don't have any calluses built for it, and you can't quite hit the notes right.

But you practice. You master every note. You turn those screeching chords into music. You practice until it becomes like second nature. You work the beat of the street until you become fluent in its ways, in its language, in its expectations, in its dangers, in its culture, in the pitch of its notes. Working the street came a bit more easily for me because I was born on those same streets, had grown into a woman on those blocks, so I skipped the novice stages of the art. But up to this point, I hadn't gone out just to engage with the people, and that felt new for a while.

Those who are best at street outreach understand everything that is happening around them, and that everything that is happening around them is doing so with a synchronicity—that the culture of survival creates a fully evolved ecosystem in these neighborhoods. It's not just you, playing your violin. There is an entire symphony playing around you, and you must become part of that orchestra. I became a part of the street. A known fixture. An instrument of the orchestra. A respected person with a presence and a reputation.

I understood the financial industry of the street. I knew which corner store would let you buy "singles" or a "loosey" cigarette instead of a whole pack, and I knew who in the neighborhood was likely to buy them. This was also the same store that allowed you to use food stamps to buy laundry detergent, an unallowable expense, by ringing up your purchase as a food product. In exchange, the store owner charged an exorbitant price for the detergent to turn a profit. I knew which stores sold weed and other drugs, and which customers frequented which establishments. These stores were part of the fabric of the neighborhood. Mostly Arab owned, the proprietors and the cashiers knew the neighbors well, exchanging pleasantries about their lives as they conducted business.

It was the same with gas station attendees, small bar owners, and more. As people live their daily lives, sitting on their porches, walking to the store, the street outreach worker has to be part of the landscape. People knew who I was, would say hello to me in passing, knew things about my family, and knew I belonged there with them as part of the social fabric of the neighborhood. I wasn't an outsider. I was a part of the natural order of things, and that status was crucial to the success of my work. I needed people to trust me with their secrets and I needed to keep my ear to the ground, because being knowledgeable keeps you safe. Knowing the neighbors, what they believe, their morals, their ethics, how they spend their time, keeps you safe. Knowing who drives in and out of the neighborhood and why keeps you safe. Knowing who may be standing outside, selling drugs, or where the drug dealer, known as "the plug" today, lives keeps you safe. Knowing who the neighborhood babysitter is, who the influential leaders of the street are, and where the neighborhood people gravitate to, particularly in times of crisis, is all important in how you conduct your business as an outreach worker.

But I hadn't penetrated the world of sex workers. I could see them, I knew what was happening, and I made sure they knew I saw them, but I wasn't yet fluent in their culture. There wasn't trust built between us yet, though they knew I was safe.

It was the end of the day and everyone had left the office, leaving me by myself to turn off the lights and lock up, when I heard the doorbell.

I opened the door and was shocked to see the dark-haired woman from the corner standing on our stoop. She asked me if I could help her, and I invited her inside.

The woman was wearing the same clothes I'd always seen her in. She was dirty and disheveled, but she walked in with some hesitancy and looked at me when she told me that it was her son's birthday. I nodded, encouraging her to continue, to which she told me that he wanted a blue cake. At first, I didn't understand. I thought maybe it had something to do with a television show for kids, a game, or that it was a type of cake I wasn't familiar with, but when she noticed my puzzled expression, the dark-haired woman went on to clarify that her son wanted a cake with blue frosting.

"Oh," I laughed nervously, "well, come on then."

I led her farther into the living room and she felt it necessary to remind me who she was.

"You know what I do for money, right?" she spat.

I nodded.

"I didn't make anything today," she followed up. She continued to tell me that she never ordered a cake for her son and was hoping I could help her.

"I think I know what we can do," a simple smile crept across my face, and I motioned for her to follow me to the kitchen.

We rummaged through all of the cabinets and I found white cake mix and white frosting. We had a lot of supplies from providing food for people in the neighborhood that needed it. Luckily, I found some blue food coloring, too. I lined all the ingredients up in front of the woman with a smile.

"Here we go," I said, watching her smirk back at me. "You can put the blue food coloring in the cake and frosting mixes and make a blue cake for him." The woman nodded, suppressing her happiness at this. I put everything in a bag and handed it to her.

The woman let me know that she appreciated my help on her way to the front door. She couldn't have done this without me.

"How old is your son?" I asked.

"Eight," she replied, sheepishly.

I saw my in. She had taken the bait of conversation, and this was my opportunity to build this experience into a relationship. I wouldn't let it slip by me.

I nodded in affirmation, "But why does he want a blue cake? I mean, that sounds like a really unique request."

The woman tightened her grip on the bag and turned to me as she neared the door, "It's his favorite color." She looked down, thinking about her son, her feelings surfacing in front of me, "He sleeps with a blue blanket and has a blue bedroom. He likes to wear blue every day, if he can."

I smiled at her, sharing in her love for her son, before pressing on. I took a moment for the ice between us to melt. "I know what you do on the street. It's not a secret," I said, staring at her directly, "and I don't care. I try not to judge people." My words made the air stiffen and felt awkward, but I had to take advantage of the moment, so I went on. "I would like to get to know you," I paused, "and help you. That is, if you could use some help."

The woman was taken aback, thinking, and all she asked was, "Why?"

"I'm a social worker. That's what I do. You've seen me around here. I'm just here to help the neighbors." I'd taken my time with my words.

She looked at me for an uncomfortable, drawn out moment before speaking. "Okay, yeah," she said.

With that, looking at this woman opening in front of me, I remembered that we had leftover Christmas gifts from our neighborhood holiday party.

"Hang on," I asked of her, holding one finger up.

She nodded. I ran upstairs and grabbed some gifts labeled for boys in her son's age group and rushed them back down, handing them to herl, "For your son."

She thanked me again and left, turning down the corner and disappearing into the evening.

The next time I saw the dark-haired woman, I took advantage of the situation instead of just driving by. I stopped and talked to her for a little while, learning that her name was Sharon. Each time I saw her, I stopped, and over time, I got closer and closer to her, eventually getting out of my car for these meetings. I spent more and more time with her on the street, in between men pulling up and leaving with her. I'd talk and laugh with Sharon about all different things and situations, and whenever she needed food, Sharon would come to the center and ask for me. She always walked away with a grocery bag full of peanut butter, bread, soup, toilet paper, and I always made sure to throw in a box of cookies for her son.

As our relationship grew and trust blossomed between us, Sharon started introducing me to other women she knew working the streets. Sharon would explain to them that I was okay and that I wasn't with the police, and before long, I was immersed in a community of women all working and selling their bodies to survive. I was learning more than I ever thought I could about an entirely foreign dimension of society. I understood poverty. I understood race and class issues. I understood the block. But this was different. Trafficking and prostitution had been hiding in plain sight all along, and my relationship to these women were my portal to enacting real and meaningful change.

As part of my master's degree program at Case, we were required to complete an internship that was not a part of our current job, so I was worried because I already had a full caseload as a case manager on the north end plus my studies to juggle. Taking on a third responsibility, separate from the world of neighborhood outreach that I already knew, seemed overwhelming. But then it dawned on me. I could use my connection to the women on the street as my internship. I would use my internship hours to learn about street prostitution, which lent me a way to continue my work with these women while also meeting the school's requirements.

This decision wouldn't come without risks and hurdles, though. I knew the school would have a problem with me engaging in what they would deem to be dangerous behavior, so I told them that I was only interacting with women who came to the center. In reality, I was going out on the street, meeting these women where they were, three days a week. I spent the other two days of the week in the library, learning what I could, but there weren't any studies about how to best help these women. In 1993, there was a surprising lack of information that did more than simply document drug and disease statistics. I learned a lot about the correlation between prostitution and HIV—there were over 177 reports and studies on this topic, as if to say that the biggest concern about prostitution was the HIV risk it posed to the good people of the rest of the world.

Young people in these studies were called "juvenile prostitutes" and were deemed "street kids" who regularly traded sex. They were written about as if anthropologists were peering into a fascinating street culture and revealing it to the world. Researchers reported that children were abused in their homes, and, as a result of this abuse, they ran away. As a way to survive, they got themselves involved in juvenile prostitution. Because the problem was defined in a linear fashion (1) abuse, (2) run away, (3) prostitution, it was seen as the child and family's problem. So the intervention became focused on the child. The child and family needed counseling and support.

Today, we know that sex trafficking is a business that involves the "supply" of victims and the "demand" of customers, sold and marketed by the traffickers. Because we've defined it that way, we now understand that we need to address supply, demand, and distribution if we are going to reduce the problem. We further understand that the adults involved should stand accountable for this tragic crime, and not children. Today, thankfully, the emphasis is on arresting the adults and providing services to youth.

My work on the street in 1993 quickly evolved, and I dove deeper and deeper. I was learning about the culture of street prostitution, the language used, about another layer of my neighborhood that I hadn't fully noticed before. I learned which houses were drug houses, who the top dope boys were, who the customers were, who was dangerous, and which cops to stay away from, because they were involved. Through it all, I was gaining a deeper understanding of the need for survival, what powerlessness truly looks and feels like, the profound effects of stigma—a stigma even I once carried, and the interpersonal assault on the self that total exclusion from the protections and privileges of society creates.

I could connect with the women on the street. Although their experiences of violence and oppression far outweighed anything I had faced, I was familiar with those feelings of stigma, disconnection, societal invisibility, and abuse. Their pain connected to my pain. By twenty-eight, I had experienced three attempted rapes and spent seven years in intimately violent relationships. I had been written off and relegated to the H.E.R.O. club, discarded as a product of poverty, and looked upon as most unlikely to succeed. I hadn't sold my body for sex in exchange for money, but I had sold my love and self-respect to violent men who, instead of money, gave me cruelty, and instead of love, gave me savagery and hatred. I, too, had lived in fear, with abuse, and grew up with the looming possibility of being exploited or hurt. My relationships with these women and this culture grew a need inside of me to learn as much as I could, to connect as deeply as possible, and to exact change in my community like no one ever had before. I wouldn't trade my love for anything else in this world again except love in return, and I wanted to offer that to the women and youth I would work with.

With my internship approved, during the next six months on the streets, I met over twenty women, about half of whom I built solid relationships with, and infiltrated the prostitution and trafficking rings of the north end of Toledo.

CHAPTER THIRTEEN
Street Prostitution

It was the early nineties, and the U.S. government hadn't recognized human trafficking as something actively happening on American soil. It wasn't until the year 2000 that the federal Trafficking Victims Protection Act would pass, and I didn't have the words yet to identify what was happening to women and youth in my community. I just knew it wasn't right. I often tell people in presentations that I didn't call it "human trafficking" at the time. Then, I simply called it "this shit ain't right," and knew something needed to be done.

The purpose of street outreach is to go where potential victims are with the goal of building meaningful relationships so as to reduce harm. I found that the best times to conduct outreach were in the morning and after five o'clock in the evening. Mornings were a good time to catch women before they'd engaged in a lot of drug use. They were more coherent, or they'd been out all night and were winding down. I also conducted street outreach in the early evening because that's when

I found the majority of women available to talk to, canvassing the block, hoping to attract men that were getting off work. Though it might seem logical, I didn't find a lot of success in trying to connect with women in late evening hours. The women were mostly really high by then and either incoherent, tweaking on crack, or I was interrupting them getting in and out of cars—interrupting the time they needed to make the bulk of their profits. Besides, the clientele late at night was different, scarier than the after five clientele.

Being that it was important for me to fit into the social fabric of the neighborhood, I had to find ways to better weave my presence into the prostitution and trafficking rings of our streets, because this was lesser-known territory to me. I knew that dressing like the neighborhood was important, and that sending workers who physically look like the people in the neighborhood you're trying to serve is important. Speaking the way they speak, eating where they eat, and being familiar with the local hangouts is all important for an outreach worker and case manager, and all of this came naturally to me when I was working with children and families in the north end. I was able to easily remove barriers and build trust because I was a part of the streets. But I wasn't a part of this new culture of prostitution and trafficking, and I knew I needed help.

Thrivers are survivors, or people who have been on the street before, have survived its hardships, and who are now strong enough to conduct outreach. They are authentic in every way, and when engaging with the women on my streets, having a thriver was a huge advantage. I started always taking a thriver with me on outreach trips, and not only were they able to help infiltrate the culture more deeply, it gave me an opportunity to help even more women. I was a supportive point of contact for her, helped keep her clean, sober, and on the right track, and she helped me get embedded into the street. We worked as a team, talking to girls on the street as well as to all of the neighbors.

Together, we drove around in my Buick, "Big Blue," talking to women on the street, visiting neighbor's houses, and touching base with different business owners around the block. People came to know Big Blue, and knew that I was around to help, not hinder them or stop their behaviors. But while they could easily identify me, my thrivers spent months teaching me how to identify working women.

It is purposely difficult for a passerby who is not interested in buying sex or cognizant of the underground world of the commercial sex trade to identify women working the streets. The sex trade in moderately sized cities is not the same as what is shown on television and in movies. Women aren't prowling street corners in neon nylons, tight skirts, and high heels. Especially in the Midwest, the scene is rarely that blatant. Working women don't stand out as such, and as a passerby, you probably wouldn't guess that they were involved in prostitution.

Looking at the street sex trade in the Midwest is like looking at a painting with repeating patterns and seeing pictures within pictures. You have to stop and stare at the painting, really analyze all of its components, to see the larger image that all of the smaller pictures make when compiled. For instance, the guy sitting on the picnic table in the park is not just a guy sitting on a table. He's the watcher, and he may occasionally deal drugs. When you watch that woman you passed walking down the street for long enough, you realize she doesn't appear to get anywhere, and she isn't carrying a purse. She's watching the passing cars. The black SUV that occasionally drives by is there to check on things and remind the trafficked victims to make their quotas, keeping them focused on their work with warnings. If you stare long enough, you'll see that SUV make several passes over time, and you'll notice how small a radius the woman you passed earlier really walks within.

When an interested driver slows down to circle the block, contemplating a purchase, looking over the merchandise, the seller will wait for the car to slow down enough for her to run over to it. But this is where her most important works starts as she begins to carefully navigate the exchange.

As she runs toward the car, the woman is looking around, making sure that law enforcement aren't around. She then engages in "chatting and checking behaviors," and leans into the car for two purposes: First, she wants to see what is in the car. Are there any weapons? She is looking in the front and backseat, glancing between the seats and the driver's legs, making sure there aren't any knives or unexpected weapons. She also checks for door handles on the passenger side of the car to make sure she can make a quick escape if she needs to. Second, while the seller is deciding whether or not to get in the car, she chats with the driver to quickly assess whether or not he is interested in an honest sex-for-money exchange. She's particularly listening to his tone, looking for any sign of agitation, and analyzing his responses to her in an attempt to reveal if he is an undercover cop. At the same time, she is paying attention to her surroundings, making sure there still aren't any police around. In addition to this complex assessment, she is simultaneously negotiating the type of sex to be purchased and the price. All of this is done in less than two minutes, before she decides to get in the car.

If the seller decides to get in the car, the next step is to determine whether she has chosen a date spot or will allow the buyer to take her to a place of his choosing. Most women on the street believe that choosing their own spot makes them safe and, therefore, more comfortable. Date sites may be chosen because they are well lit with people in close proximity. Of course, these sites provide an increased risk that someone will call the police. However, dark spots away from people increase the risk that violence may occur. Although, once crack cocaine hit the streets in the eighties and nineties, and now heroin in modern times, these assessments are still completed but the decision to get in the car has changed. Women who are drug addicted are likely to get in the car regardless of the result of their assessment. And instead of using the assessment to determine her decision to go through with the sale, it is more commonly used to assess the risk for danger so that she knows how alert she needs to be.

Early in my outreach, I met Tonia. Initially, Tonia was ardent about her chatting and checking ritual, and she was one of the key women who taught me about these types of safety measures and how to watch for them. Unfortunately, over time, like many who work the streets, Tonia became drug addicted and stopped declining dates, even when there were red flags signaling danger. Tonia still took her dates to a spot where she felt vaguely safe for sex, but one night, one of her customers said he'd be willing to score her drugs, saying they could spend the night in a motel, getting high and having sex. Seeing no indication that he was potentially dangerous, Tonia agreed.

The man bought an eight ball of crack cocaine, which is roughly 3.5 grams. They first stopped at convenience store to buy a single fake rose—the kind they sell near the counter. People throw away the rose and use the glass tubing in the stem to smoke crack with. Then, he rented a room at a motel on Telegraph Road, just over the Michigan state line. The motel was one-story high, off the side of the road, with a gravel parking lot that housed only three other cars.

Once they entered the room, both Tonia and the man took off their clothes, had sex, and began smoking crack. Hours into their rendezvous, the man started to get paranoid. Tonia noticed him staring at her for long periods of time, making her uncomfortable. The room filled with an awkward tension that alerted Tonia to danger.

"What's up?" she asked as she hit the pipe.

The man stared back at her for a moment before replying, "You wanna put my money back in my wallet?" He accused her of an impossible crime.

Tonia explained to the man that she hadn't taken any money from him, and this was clearly evident since she was nude. But he just sat at the edge of the bed and continued to stare at her. The longer he stared, the stranger she came to feel. Trying not to appear scared or vulnerable, Tonia started to raise her voice and gather her clothes, all while denying that she had taken any money from him. Tonia dressed herself while the man stared at her, turned to the door and started to leave when the man jumped up, grabbed her, and threw her down on the bed. The man straddled her and started beating her. Tonia tried to fight back, but he was too strong and continued punching her before finally strangling her. Desperately, she tried to peel his fingers from around her throat, and when that failed, she tried to buck him off of her body. He was too heavy. She tried scratching and digging at his face, but she felt herself growing weaker. Tonia recalls looking at the man and then looking past him and to the ceiling. She remembers having a conversation in her head about giving up, praying that her death would be quick, resigning herself to the seemingly inevitable. She was going to die, and maybe that would be okay because she could finally stop fighting—she could finally be at peace.

As those thoughts of relinquishment and relief swirled around her mind, another voice forced its way through—a more powerful and resolute voice. "Fight back!" the voice encouraged. "You're going to live," this loud and booming presence yelled at her. "It's not your time," she heard atop all the chaos. Thinking she was dead or greatly incapacitated, Tonia's perpetrator loosened his grip. When that happened, Tonia summoned the strength to push the man off of her. She pulled her feet up, wedging them between their bodies, and kicked the man off the bed before running to the door.

Before Tonia could make it out, a stronger fight ensued. The man grabbed at her, both of them punching and kicking, all while she reached for the door handle. When the door swung open, the man released Tonia, exposed, seeing the other cars parked in the lot. Looking around, Tonia noticed the motel office in the distance. The door was open with a lit sign in the window. Tonia dropped to the ground, bereft of strength, and crawled across the gravel lot. As she pulled her body the distance, rocks scraped her knees, leaving a spotted red trail behind her. But she made it. Tonia crawled all the way to safety.

This incident drove Tonia to her breaking point, and she cleaned up her act. I saw Tonia the next Thanksgiving, selling frozen turkeys at a grocery store counter. She smiled at me as I approached and we hugged.

"I'm doing good," Tonia assured me, and I could tell she was by her demeanor. Tonia went on to tell me about all the progress she'd made since we'd last met, and I made sure to let her know how proud I was of her and that I'd always be a support and resource for her. These types of encounters, seeing women and teens doing well for themselves and making progress, are always the best holiday gifts.

CHAPTER FOURTEEN
Hidden in Plain Sight

The work I was doing with the women on the street didn't always impress the neighbors. They didn't get to see the small moments or the big victories these women were making. They were just sick of prostitution infiltrating their neighborhood, and I could understand that. So it was important that I made my impact on the local sex trade very clear and apparent to them, because to them, I was simply part of the problem, cozying up to prostitutes, keeping them healthy and supporting their work.

On three different occasions, we were asked to attend the neighborhood watch meeting with an array of members of the community to discuss prostitution in the neighborhood. Some of the neighbors were angry that we were "helping" the women and argued that when they called the police, women who were arrested were back on the street the next day or even the same day. They were angry that their children had to play in areas where they had to sweep up condoms, and I could relate to that because I, too, had run out of my house to sweep up relics of the night before to make space for my daughter, or chase away a car parked out front at night, trying to engage in a sex trade transaction.

Through a lot of deep and empathetic communication, we finally obtained an understanding with the neighbors when we explained to them that women on the street were arrested, on average, ten times while involved—that they were arrested, given a court date, and then didn't appear. After so many charges, women would be held overnight, arraigned in the morning, asked their plea, to which they plead, "Not guilty," and were then given another court date for which they wouldn't appear. This process was costing the city around $2,000 each time a woman was caught in this nonsensical cycle. Before long, many women working the street had racked up so many arrests and warrants for "failure to appear" in court that they were being picked up and shipped off to serve eight or more months in the regional jail. And when their time was served, where were they supposed to go? It was inevitable for them to repeat this cycle.

We told the neighbors that until the law was changed, we were working to build relationships with these women in order to help them transition into drug treatment programs and other services. With these resources ready and available, we would be the necessary bridge that helped women to move from the streets into substance abuse treatment, housing, and case management. Over time, some women might not return to the streets at all. We also explained that, yes, we were investing in harm reduction for these women, because our first goal was to save lives, but ultimately, that prevented the neighbors from finding dead women in their streets.

But most importantly, these women had families. There was someone in the world who missed their daughter, their sister, or their mother. There was someone carrying around a tear-stained picture of this person in their wallet, looking at a framed picture on a wall, and longing for this loved person back. But addiction is strong and calls women into prostitution to feed a habit. They are being prostituted by drugs, poverty, and earlier trauma, or being forced into prostitution by a pimp. These experiences were too strong for victims to simply walk away from. When I had their attention, I made sure to make it known that the neighbors, the women in prostitution, and myself all had one thing in common: we all knew the police and city government were ineffectual in meeting our needs, that the school systems were substandard, that our neighborhoods were invisible, that the legal system in place to deal with prostitution had only made things worse, so they agreed that our work was important because it might at least help. And like proper social workers, we also provided the neighbors with resources and support programs, because they deserved our guidance, too.

We continued our work in the north and south ends of Toledo. We drove around or, on some days, walked Lagrange Street. We had to go where the vulnerable and invisible were—had to meet them on their turf if we were ever going to make a real difference. We always talked to women one-on-one about how they were doing, making sure we went over safe practices with them. I never left without giving them something to keep them safe and healthy, be it condoms, sandwiches, juice, or printed information about where to find safe shelter, a meal, and mental health and substance abuse services. We also gave out information about "dangerous dates" or men who were known to rape or hurt women. All of our work was in the name of safety, to reduce harm and create a pathway for women to get off the streets and into recovery and housing, if they wanted to. That's the most important thing to understand: I was always going to do what I could to keep them safe, but it wasn't my responsibility or my place to coerce them out of their way of life. They had to want help.

I started receiving reports of a serial rapist frequenting the north end. Three separate women informed me that they'd gotten into a car with the passenger door handle removed, rendering escape impossible. One woman said that once she noticed this, she began fighting her customer. As the car swerved and came to a stop, the woman worked her way over the seat and into the back, escaping through the back door. Because they were on a semi-busy street, he drove off. A second report came from a woman who said a man tried to drive her to the outskirts of town. When she asked him to take her to a busier part of town, he refused. Trapped because the door handle was missing, the man took her to a wooded area where he raped her. She also eventually made her way to the backseat and escaped into the woods. The third woman recounted kicking the passenger door until it flew open and jumping from the moving vehicle to get away. Because of these stories, I notified the police and made a "dangerous date" flyer, posting them up and down Lagrange Street and along east side and south end neighborhoods.

I spent the next summer conducting outreach in Big Blue with my friend and survivor-thriver, Marcea. Marcea had worked hard and clawed her way all the way out from being trafficked, crack addicted, and a street worker to obtaining her chemical dependency license and becoming the director of a local substance abuse program for women. I had a lot of respect for Marcea.

Marcea was abused as a child, and she was first trafficked by a man her mother knew when she was a teenager. Not knowing how to properly channel the trauma, she self-medicated through repeated drug use. She became drug addicted and subsequently used sex trading on the street to obtain money to maintain her drug addiction. Marcea's trafficker sold her all around the state and into other states. Once, while she was working a truck stop near Detroit, two police officers pulled up and asked her what she was doing. Because of the precarious situation, she immediately confessed to them that she was "working." They arrested her and put her in the back of their car. The police told her that if she had sex with both of them that they would allow her to work the rest of the day. She did. Much to Marcea's surprise, the officers returned later that day and had sex with her again, again allowing her to work additional hours. This only served to teach Marcea that customers come in all shapes, sizes, and professions, and it taught her to be distrustful of those there to help.

Of all the street savvy women, Marcea was among the best. She knew the potential terror that could be found on the street and she was hypervigilant in looking out for it. By the time I met Marcea, she had been sober and had not been sex trafficked or in prostitution for some time. The one thing that struck me about Marcea was that she was a no-nonsense type of woman. She was a stunning, dark skinned, African-American woman. She was a spiritual woman, too, which always puzzled me. After hearing her story, I couldn't imagine that this woman could be so close to God. Her most terrifying experience came when she was approached by a man that purchased sex with her. He wanted her to have sex with him and a friend. He told her to meet him around the corner and gave her an address. So as to not create suspicion, the man told Marcea to wait for a few minutes before coming around the corner. She did. After a time, she walked up to the door and knocked. When the man opened the door, Marcea knew to quickly scan the room before stepping in, making sure it was safe. The room was dark with only one lamp, so she couldn't see clearly, but Marcea counted more than four men in the room.

Marcea looked up at the man's face, standing at the doorway, waving her in. In that moment, she knew something was terribly wrong. Instead of stepping into the room, Marcea turned and began to run. As she was running, she could hear the men piling out of the house, one of them shouting, "Get that bitch!" Others were screaming for her to come back. One man told another one to, "Go get the car," and another instructed, "Run the bitch over." Marcea's heart pounded in her chest as she ran, all while looking for a place to hide.

Marcea recounts that there was a little boy on a bike, riding in the street. He rode up to her and casually warned her, saying, "Hey lady, they said they are going to run you over! Go and hide on that porch!" The boy pointed to a grey, dingy two-story house that looked abandoned. The porch was enclosed. As fast as she could, Marcea ran up onto the porch and ducked down. The car full of men drove by, looking for her. Marcea was quiet and patient, sweating with anxiety, until the men eventually left. When she emerged from the porch, the little boy was also gone. Marcea never saw him again. Unfortunately, this incident was not enough to keep Marcea off the street. Her addiction and the effects of her trauma kept her chained to street work.

As some women do, Marcea became pregnant while on the street, battling her demons through sex work and drug addiction. Not knowing who the father was, she maintained the pregnancy. In the wake of such a monumental experience, Marcea disconnected from her reality—she wanted the baby. Marcea wanted the baby to be happy and healthy, and for her life to be happy and healthy, but her lifestyle didn't afford this sort of privilege. Putting it to the back of her mind, hoping for a way to transition into a more normal version of life as a mother, time passed. Each day, the gestational age of the baby grew, and she tried to slow down her drug use for the sake of the baby. But she kept selling sex. In fact, Marcea realized she could make more money as a pregnant woman who was lactating. She used this money for drugs and food, telling herself all the while to just use enough drugs to keep her body functioning. She didn't have prenatal care.

Already feeling worthless and duped into believing in love as a teenager, only to have it twisted and distorted by a trafficker, Marcea occasionally fantasized about the life she wanted, especially with the growing life inside her belly. This often sent her spiraling into a deeper sense of depression and worthlessness. Somewhere deep down, she knew that, each day, she was destroying life instead of creating it.

Marcea's son was born with symptoms related to her crack addiction, but much to her surprise, she was allowed to take him home. She didn't own anything besides a room with a bed and a dresser. Marcea pulled out the dresser drawer and made a bed for her son. After placing him in the dresser, Marcea slid to the floor and cried endlessly. It was all real now. She was a mother. And for the last nine months, part of her felt like the pregnancy was a fantasy, and she fully expected him to be taken from her at birth, so seeing her baby now, feeling the gravity of this new responsibility, was overwhelming.

After long hours of emotional contemplation, Marcea made a decision. She called child protective services on herself and told them that she wasn't fit to parent him. She told me that she had always given in to her needs, but this was one time she felt compelled to nurture the needs of another—of her innocent son. That day was a turning point. After turning her baby over to authorities, Marcea admitted herself into treatment.

After years of hard work and perseverance, Marcea was able to get her son back. She was gifted with the opportunity to raise him, to change her life in exchange for offering her son a better life, and she shared with me that her son graduated high school with honors.

After my experiences with Marcea, I began to ask women in my research studies if they were spiritual or had some sort of religious affiliation. Over 90% of the women and youth I have reached in my twenty-five years of practice identify as having a connection to God or some presence bigger than themselves. I go back and forth between rationalizing that, because, of course, these women and youth have had horrific experiences and no one to turn to except someone or something unseeable—something bigger than themselves. Of course women with tragic experiences have no one to believe in and no one to call on, so they call on the "big guns" to help them out of a situation that seems impossible or when they are provided with a gift of survival that they feel they don't deserve. *It must be God doing this,* they think.

Or maybe it is God who is driving me to this work and providing women and youth with the safety and support they need right when they need it. But my puzzlement is and will always be the age-old conundrum that God can't be all loving and be all powerful at the same time. Why would an all-loving God who has all of the power allow such tragedies to occur in the world? I've received explanations that God is teaching, God is punishing, or that we can't understand everything about God. These explanations seem weak and unsatisfactory. But I leave the theology to the people that study it and continue on with my work.

CHAPTER FIFTEEN
Seeking Refuge

Where Bancroft Street intersects with Franklin is a darker part of town, and Marcea and I were patrolling these streets on a sunny afternoon, looking to reach out to any women in need. Just ahead was a small grassy field—a vacant plot left from the demolition of a few condemned houses. We saw a short, thin African-American woman weaving her way through the cut when Marcea leaned forward, trying to get a better look at her.

"I know her," Marcea said, squinting and peering. I pulled the car up and slowed, eyeing the woman. She looked familiar to me, but I couldn't quite place her face.

Marcea rolled down her window, "Hey, come over here for a minute," she called to the woman.

The woman turned around, revealing to us her small frame, dark skin, and big, pretty round eyes. She looked to be in her late thirties, and was skittish at first. The woman walked over to the car, but stopped short of being in reach.

"Don't you remember me?" Marcea quickly started in. The woman just stared. "From Lagrange Street? And you went to the hospital? I visited you every day."

The woman inched a little closer to the car.

Marcea continued, "I'm so glad you're alright. You were really hurt, for real." The woman continued to stare at us. With a compassionate tone, Marcea asked the woman to get in the car. "We want to talk to you."

Quietly, the woman got in the backseat. Not knowing this particular scene well enough, I drove a few blocks down and parked where I could see the landscape from a safe vantage point. Normally at this point, I give every woman I meet for the first time a similar spiel. I tell them who I am, why I'm there, and that I'm not judging them, that I just want to help them be safe on the street. But Marcea spoke to this woman with familiarity, like they were still on the street, in it, together.

"So you don't remember at all?" Marcea asked, peering around the passenger seat into the back. The woman stared back at her, clearly trying to access some memory, when she must have had a flash of recollection because her eyes began to water. Unexpectedly, the woman reached around the seat and hugged Marcea. I watched the woman's memories flood in, and she embraced Marcea with fondness for several moments.

My curiosity and my heart needed to know about their relationship. "How do you two know each other?" I asked. Marcea looked at me and then back to the woman.

"You remember you were on Lagrange Street?" Marcea asked the woman again.

"Yes."

Marcea looked between us both. "This is Layla. When I was out there working the street, I was walking down Lagrange, about three in the morning. No one was out. It was as quiet and dead out there as it can get. You know how it can be. It had just rained and so the sidewalk and the street were still wet and all I could hear was my own shoes clicking. I walked past this alley and I heard this thumping noise kinda far away, and sort of a deep guttural sound that followed each thump. I passed the alley, but then backed up to look down the alley again. I could barely see because the streetlight on the corner was the only form of light. I saw something. It looked like a man near a dumpster. He had one hand on the metal dumpster and he was using it to help him maintain his balance as he jumped up and down violently on something. Each time he came down, there was a thump followed by a guttural moan. He was jumping up and down on you."

Marcea turned to me then and said, "I was witnessing a murder. This man was trying to kill her."

As soon as Marcea walked farther down the alley, she was so scared that she was almost tip-toeing. Taking careful steps as she approached, she realized what was happening and yelled, "Hey, what are you doing?" The man turned to look at her and then ran away.

She told Layla, "So, I ran up to you. I knelt down to help you and you started swinging wildly. I ran out of the alley, found someone, and they called the police."

Marcea went on to describe that she couldn't identify Layla's nose or eyes or any of the prominent features of her face to police. They were swollen and full of blood. When the rescue team appeared, Marcea disappeared out of the alley and went on her way. She was a known prostitute with a warrant, and to avoid jail, Marcea left the scene. But Marcea was haunted by what that man had done to the woman she found. It was a tragic reminder that there are men in the world who look for women like that to unleash their hatred and violence on. It haunted Marcea so badly that she later went to St. Vincent's Hospital to visit the woman she'd saved. Marcea visited Layla every day for five days. She asked Layla if she remembered her visits.

"Do you remember? You had tubes coming out of your mouth and your head. They had you hooked up to wires everywhere. Your head was swollen twice its size. Your eyes were swollen shut. You had stitches across your face. I was on drugs so bad that I was skinny, I smelled, and I was so embarrassed to go and visit you, but I did because I didn't want you to be alone, and when anybody showed up, I disappeared. Do you remember that?"

I could see Marcea's eyes tearing up. She saw herself in Layla and if she couldn't save herself at that time, she would save someone else. I thought about my own attempted rapes. I thought about all of the women at my mother's kitchen table through the years that talked about the violence they'd experienced. Earning your seat at my mother's table to talk about your experience with violence seemed like a rite of passage. It wasn't the start of your period that made you a woman on my street. It wasn't your Bat Mitzvah, your Quinceañera, or your Debutante Ball. It was your ability to experience and survive violence. I thought about my own violent relationships. Most women experience some sort of emotional violence, whether it be through our personal lives or through the repeated media messages that tell us we are too fat, too dark, too old, or too something that isn't quite right. We walk around insecure and never happy with ourselves.

Is violence a woman's experience? If so, why do we speak of it in terms of someone else's experience? Does it transcend race, age, and class? We say, "Those victims of domestic violence," or, "Those victims of rape," but when we also assess the emotional violence we all suffer, it seems that violence IS a woman's experience. When we allow violence to be separated, sorted out, measured, and individually named, we don't allow our collective experience to be recognized.

Layla shook her head, telling Marcea she didn't remember any of it. Layla knew her truth was staring her in the face—that her life could be taken at a moment's notice without a large investigation or a cry from a family or community for justice—and she began to cry.

I could feel my eyes water. Three black women in a car, trying to help each other do more than just survive the violence of men, but to thrive. Was the world ready to give women like us the opportunity to live free from violence? That experience affected me deeply. As we talked, Layla admitted she hadn't felt safe going to the police or going to counseling to address that trauma. She wouldn't pursue justice of any kind through the courts. She knew she wouldn't be taken seriously. In the end, Layla's story was just another story from the street—the same story that so many women experience, but have to live with, broken and often in silence. No crime reported. No counseling. No loving support from friends or family. No justice for women like her. Layla lived every day with the psychological trauma and physical aftermath of what happened. Like many women in her situation, Layla didn't have other options, and though Marcea saved Layla's life that one night, there were many nights to come that Layla would have to survive.

Violence is a critical component of commercial sexual exploitation. Women on the street are less likely to report brutal felonies, like what Layla experienced, to the police for fear they will be judged and charged with committing a misdemeanor, such as prostitution. They don't bother going through the charade of a justice system that isn't committed to serving them equally.

Prosecutors build their reputation and careers on winnable cases. Women in prostitution don't often make for sympathetic victims to a jury or even a judge. In fact, earlier reports of rape victims, in which the victim was a known prostitute, were sometimes recorded as an NHI (No Human Involved) case. NHI was reported to have started before the seventies among police officers who would refer to prostitute rape victims as "NHI," signifying that the person they should help was not even worthy of personhood because they had such a low social status.

Addicted to crack cocaine, homeless, and without a soul in the world to support her, Marcea worked the streets day-in and day-out, getting in cars with whomever pulled over and paid her, knowing each time that her life was in danger. As I looked at each one of us, teary eyed, in the car, I thought about where we'd all come from and what we'd each endured. Marcea cried with relief that Layla had survived, and with gratitude that she herself had been able to turn her own life around. Layla cried reflecting on her life and her many brushes with death. I cried because of their experiences and for the grace given to me that spared me from this life. We all cried together for a larger reason—for how women, especially women of color, are treated in America, for a system of oppression that keeps the American dream out of their reach, and for a million other girls on the streets, just trying to survive. I was witnessing the emotion of two women who had to once protect each other, who weren't privileged enough to be kept safe under the protections of society. I cried for the broken little girl inside of me who kept me motivated to do this work, knowing that I'd come so close, so many times, to living Layla's life. We felt it together, that something bigger than us needed to change.

It was the nineties, and there weren't any movements actively exposing sexual assault, outing the Bill Cosby's and Harvey Weintstein's of the world. We weren't on the verge of any feminist revolution of this sort. There wasn't a "me too" and a "time's up" movement to combat the abuse of women. There weren't any abolitionist marches or pro sex worker groups that were powerful and vocal enough to reach the north end of Toledo. We were just three black women, sitting in a car, realizing in a moving moment that we had no recourse through which to air our grievances and fully participate in a just and fair society. And then it dawned on me.

I knew Layla. I realized why she looked so familiar. She went to my high school. In an instant, I was able to see past the years of abuse on Layla's face and body, and I remembered that small girl being bullied in class the way I had been. I didn't want to risk embarrassing her, didn't want her to know that I remembered her suffering or the potential she once had.

We spent the next hour with Layla in the car, listening to her recount the horror story that was her childhood. She'd been brought up in foster care and through the juvenile court system. She told us about the number of times she ran away, the number of rapes and abuses she suffered. As she told us her story, she was deadpan in her delivery, which I often found to be the case with women who worked the street. It was too easy for them to tell me that they had been raped, or that they had to flee a moving vehicle to escape a dangerous customer, or that their uncle started violating them when they were just three years old. A lifetime of complex traumas and dissociation dulls the senses and eats away at any real emotional response. Women like Layla were mere shadows of themselves in the wake of unspeakable pain—pain that they'd learned to endure long before they took to the streets.

We talked about recovery and trust. We bonded. When it was time to leave, we left Layla with our phone numbers, asking her to promise to reach out if she ever needed anything. If she were ever ready to change her life, we would be ready to help her. I drove away, leaving Layla in her circumstance. That's the hardest part of street outreach. Driving away. All you want to do is take them in your car, make them believe their life can be different, and put them in a treatment program with trauma counseling so they can begin their recovery. But doing that, even for the right reasons, is a form of control. Making someone do something against their will is anti-freedom. And if trafficking and being prostituted by drugs is a form of modern day slavery, where a trafficker or drug controls you, then freedom is the appropriate response. I won't be a person who takes another's choice away, even if I think it's for the best. When I left Layla, I was feeling both hope and loss. I was overwhelmed. *What could I do about women like Layla?* I felt frustrated. I didn't have the answers, nor the power I thought I needed. All I could do was offer some support, but I felt like I was emptying the ocean with a teaspoon.

Layla was found dead in the trunk of an abandoned car just three months later. Once in a while, I look at Layla's high school photo and wonder what she'd be doing if this hadn't happened to her and what her children would be doing. I wonder how she might have contributed to her neighborhood and community if her experiences had been different. Her memory reminds me of why this work is so important. Layla never deserved her fate.

Meeting Layla and dealing with her death made me think about my childhood friends. I knew many of the girls I'd loved were out there, somewhere, and I'd heard some stories about Emma Kay. Stories like Layla's and Marcea's are the dark reality for any street outreach worker. Your days are spent wading through tragedy after tragedy, carrying some beacon of hope for those that don't have any left. Shortly after the news of Layla's death, the local news ran a story about the work I was doing, and it had people talking.

If you want to know how you're doing in the community, people will tell you. Even today, I have past friends, acquaintances, and random strangers who recognize me and walk up to tell me exactly how I'm doing and what they think. Most all of it has been positive and encouraging with people thanking me for what I'm doing, expressing they never knew there was such a big problem like this. *Bless you, you are in my prayers.* Occasionally, I also hear other comments, like, "Why are you wasting your career on this?" or, "You could be at a big, prestigious university. Why stay in Toledo?" and, "You can't make people do what they don't want to do. Those people want to be out there." I hear the latter less and less. I just smile and say, "Thanks for looking out for me, and, yes, those women and children are worth it."

I love running into people from my old north end neighborhood because they usually beam with pride in being part of the north end tribe. They typically say things like, "I saw you on the news and I told my wife, 'Hey, that's Celia! I know her. We use to go to school together!'" My favorite comments come from my own black people, because they will tell you exactly how you're doing, no holds barred. They will tell you the truth, give you suggestions, and pray with you right there in the middle of the grocery store. Even though it's awkward, I love the support.

People always wonder how I can stay in this type of work, why I try to do the impossible, often for the ungrateful, and the answer is both simple and complicated: It's daunting. It's depressing. And it's mostly tragic. Advocates in my line of work often suffer vicarious traumas and burnout—the crippling emotional residue from bearing witness to the pain, fear, and terror that others have suffered. Some people become hardened and struggle to relate to that pain and fear. Some people self-destruct under the pressure and start to self-medicate to numb themselves at the end of the day, and I've been there and back. It can get hard to quiet the stories of those you serve from re-playing in your mind, and sometimes it's hard to sleep.

At one point, I found myself beginning to drown in hatred—hatred for what men will do to women, for what women sometimes do to other women, but mostly for what women will do to themselves. But in the end, I do this work, day-in and day-out, because I can. There aren't enough people in the world with the heart and stomach, by no fault of their own, capable of doing this work. In so many ways, society has created a heinous problem that is much larger than all of us on multiple and complicated levels, and there are very few of us with the skills or the tools to combat it, so I am driven and compelled by the fact that I have a chance at enacting real and honest change by directly addressing it.

But that drive didn't come simply. Beyond growing up in an underserved neighborhood with little protection from abuse and neglect, having been raised and immersed in the cultures capable of molding and shaping women into street workers, laden with trafficking and drug-induced violence, there was a shift that took place within me in the nineties. As I dove deeper and deeper into street work, especially after facing the deaths of women, and seeing the battered faces and hearts of my victimized friends, I desperately needed to find hope and meaning to keep myself from spiraling into disillusion and pessimism, so I began to choose to focus on the successes instead of the tragedies. I am continually inspired by those women and girls who are changing their lives one small success at a time.

Today, after a long journey of learning how to align my emotional health and my perspective, I absolutely love walking into a meeting, whether I'm a visitor, a member, or the lead, and looking over all of the advocates at the table—front line workers, politicians, directors of agencies—all there to combat trafficking and inch the movement forward. That is my Picasso. It's the most beautiful painting I've ever seen. That is my drug, and I am totally addicted.

CHAPTER SIXTEEN
Common Ground

At the end of a six-month period of street work, I called a meeting with the women I knew and asked them to tell me about the type of services they needed or that other women like them might need. With all of the violence and danger surrounding them, I needed to get more specific in my work, and I wanted to provide them the resources and care that they wanted, not what anyone else thought they needed. We brainstormed together for a couple of hours while I wrote down all of their thoughts. In 1993, we had created a program together, and all of their needs and suggestions embodied the components of this new program. I asked them to think of a name for this program, and they settled on the name "Second Chance," believing that everyone deserves a second chance at life. By the end of our session together, I had the framework for what would become the Second Chance program, the first anti-trafficking program in Ohio.

Second Chance was built as an individualized case management program, meaning we would assess women to determine their needs and then each woman would decide on the things she wanted to work on. The services were intensive, comprehensive, and flexible enough to meet each woman's needs. Our weekly support and psychosocial groups became so valuable to the women that some would have their customers drop them off for group. One woman even convinced her trafficker that coming to group was mandated as a condition of her probation. I was thrilled that the women believed the group was valuable, and as we worked to maintain the comradery and support they received, it was my hope that some of them would internalize enough of the messaging from group that they would be empowered to reach out to me for more help and make bigger life changes. And many did.

If I had to sum up the work I did with women and youth in the jails, in juvenile detention, on the street, in courts, and in groups, my main message to the women I worked with was that I cared. I repeated this message in many different ways and showed them that I cared by being there in ways that empowered them to think about their life, their past, and the potential for their future. I worked to be as authentic and nonjudgmental as I could in delivering this message. I let them know when I was frustrated, and I invited them to share their true feelings about their experiences and how they felt. When they made small strides, I let them know how proud I was. We celebrated with certificates and lunches. I would empower them. If or when they needed a mother figure, a sister, a mentor, a friend, I wasn't their social worker, I filled that need. If they needed to talk, to cry, to feel frustrated, or to feel angry, we felt it together and talked through it. When they were feeling brave, I pushed them to think about the possibility of having the future they dreamed about. When they were feeling lost, I asked that they trust in themselves. When they were feeling depressed, I offered them my support, linked them with a therapist, or asked them to call on their newfound group of sisters for support.

In the truest spirit of a social worker, I met women and youth where they were at psychologically, socially, and emotionally. I linked them to services as much as I could, and when they were afraid or intimidated to go, I went with them. I hugged them when they needed it. They had my personal phone number. I worried more about having boundaries that kept us both emotionally healthy and less about professional boundaries that kept us separated. When they fell into old habits and tried to manipulate me, I reminded them of who I was and what I knew about the game. When they relied on me way too much, I taught them how to depend more on the group of women as well as themselves.

During this time, I was learning in school about various experiments and studies that had a significant impact on human behavior. One was the blue eyed, brown eyed experiment. In 1968, Jane Elliott was an elementary school teacher. The day after Martin Luther King, Jr. died, she went into her classroom and conducted an experiment. She told the brown eyed students that they were less than the blue eyed students. They were more greedy, more needy, and overall not as good as the blue eyed students. Jane slowly watched the brown eyed students diminish in affect. She watched their mood grow more somber. They didn't do as well as the blue eyed students on tests and during activities. They weren't as happy.

Soon, she changed the experiment and told the brown eyed students they were special and the blue eyed students were not as good. She watched the brown eyed students flourish in their mood, affect, testing, and participation. She saw them excel, while she saw the exact opposite in the blue eyed students. She further saw the way each type of student looked at and treated one another.

Additional experiments like this have taken place, and, each time, those that were told they were less than and then stigmatized by authority acted exactly as they were treated. They didn't rise above the stigma, but instead fulfilled the expectation. I used this information, and indeed everything I learned in my classes, to help me as I worked with the women. I became a strengths-based worker, looking for and seeing strengths in the women and helping them to build on those and become empowered.

One of my referrals at this time was Virginia. Virginia was a thirty-two-year-old, beautiful, brown-toned African-American woman living in the north end. She had two elementary school-aged children. When we began working together, Virginia's goal was to complete an associate's degree. I encouraged her and supported her dream by providing transportation, arranging babysitting for her two girls, and helping her with her homework when she needed it. She enrolled at the University of Toledo and began taking classes. We spent quite a bit of time together. Virginia even helped me run my group for mothers. When she needed food or clothes, she came down to the center and got what she needed. Her two children came to the center for tutoring and participated in our after school programs and played in our gym. It was a great fit.

Virginia had been addicted to drugs and, as a result, was adamant about attending her Alcoholics Anonymous (AA) meetings. What I didn't know was when classes started getting tough that Virginia would skip her AA meetings to finish her homework instead. When her children needed her attention, she skipped a meeting to make sure she met their needs. After a year of schooling, Virginia made a fatal mistake. Instead of using recognizing she needed to slow down or take a break from school, she walked to the local bar near her house to blow off some steam. Just one night of drinking, she told herself, and then she would get right back to her studies and parenting. Virginia felt like needed to cut loose and release some stress.

But drinking led to smoking crack. She met a guy somewhere that night. No one knows for sure if he was at the bar or if she met him along the way, but they ended up back at Virginia's house, where he beat and strangled her to death. He stuffed Virginia's body in her closet and fled.

The next morning, I drove up to Virginia's house. Her two girls were sitting on the stoop, waiting. I rolled down the window to ask about their mom.

"We're waiting for our mom to come home," the ten-year-old said. "We stayed across the street at Ms. Pearl's house last night so Mommy could go out."

Despite having their hats and coats on, I had them get in my car to keep warm. After waiting a while, I ended up telling the girls to go back to Ms. Pearl's house and wait for their mom to come home. I watched as they entered and the door to Ms. Pearl's closed. I didn't think much about it until I was called into James' office. He told me that Virginia was dead and he gave me the news about where she was found.

Virginia's children went to stay with their grandmother, who went on to raise them. After Virginia died, I spent almost a week in bed, mourning her death and thinking about her two little girls. I felt like the work I was doing was meaningless. Virginia's death and all of the women and kids before her made me feel hopeless. No matter what I did, it wasn't enough. *As a social worker, am I supposed to just help do what I can? And then when it doesn't work out, am I supposed to just let it go and move on to the next client? Am I supposed to just help each person as best I can and that's it?*

> *It wasn't good enough. We needed laws changed. We needed to increase awareness and improve the dignity and respect of all people. We needed to decrease stigma. We needed to better understand what was happening in our communities. But I had absolutely no idea how to get that done, and I didn't have the authority to do any of it. I needed a doctorate so that I could affect change on a policy level and on a research level. I needed to reach a status that provided a platform where people might listen. I no longer wanted to work one-on-one. I didn't want to help one, I wanted to help the many.*

Crack cocaine had taken over the streets, much like heroin has today. All of the protective factors that women employed were now being subverted. The need for the drug was so strong that women opted to get into almost any car that would stop, whether they had an uneasy feeling about it or not. Some women became slaves to the crack house, taking up residence there and providing any type of sex that dope boys wanted.

The sex was often degrading, and the women were used to entertain the concocted fantasies of the men of the house.

With this change in the dynamic of the street, many women were disappearing into crack dens and being subjected to dangerous and life-threatening practices. One of the women I worked with, Tesa, had been missing for a while. When I noticed her long absence, I started asking about her and looking for her on the street. I even searched for her across treatment programs in the hopes that maybe she'd pursued help. Finally, I ran into her. Tesa let me know that she had been kept in the basement of a crack house and fed drugs, tied to a dirty mattress, for men to come and engage in vile sexual acts with her. She escaped by waiting for everyone to leave, chewing her ropes and breaking a basement window and climbing out. The irony, though, is that once Tesa freed herself, she was back on the street the same day.

"I know it's crazy, huh? I worked to get myself free, and the same day, found a date and bought some dope," Tesa confessed to me that the power of her addiction trapped her in the cycles of violent street work.

Because this occasionally happened to the women I knew, sometimes, I was forced to look for them in places I never wanted to go. After catching up with her some time back, my Appalachian friend, Jeanie, continued working with me through outreach. We met regularly, so when I hadn't seen her for a couple of weeks, I started to worry. I knew that she was addicted to crack, and with the current climate of sex work becoming so deeply entangled with the drug trade, I knew where I needed to look for a missing woman first this time.

Alerted about a location from one of my contacts on the street,

I pulled up to a house in the north end that looked abandoned, save a few bikers loitering in the backyard. I went in broad daylight, so I had a clear view of a corner of the yard, with three-quarters of the yard being blocked by the house. I sat in my car for a while, watching the scene and listening to discern the number of voices I could overhear in the back. I could only make out two voices talking. I could see one of the voices attached to a tall, slender man wearing a sleeveless denim biker jacket with a logo on the back. He had shoulder-length brown hair, a mustache, and was holding a beer. With as much information as I could gather through observation from the street, I got out of my car and walked to the front door.

When I knocked, no one answered, so I started to walk around to the back of the house. The backyard was small with patches of grass peeking out of the dirt. There were two dilapidated lawnchairs and a garbage can full of empty beer bottles and cans. The man I saw from my car had gotten up and walked over to a tree in the back of the yard to relieve himself. The man I couldn't see walked around the side of the house to where I was.

"Who the fuck are you?" he demanded, surprised to see me in the backyard.

I told him my name and that I was looking for Jeanie and asked if he'd seen her. Because I was from the north end, I knew that when walking into a potentially dangerous situation that you have to act like you belong there. I called on my roots.

The man looked me over before responding, "Yeah, she's in the house," and then left around the side.

The second man finished his business and turned around from the tree to face me, seemingly surprised to know that Jeanie was in the house.

When I repeated that I was looking for Jeanie, the first man yelled out to the house, "Hey Jeanie, somebody's here to see ya." He motioned toward the back door.

There were two steps missing to the back porch, so I took a long step up to the concrete slab serving as a porch. The back door was chock full of chipped, peeling paint on the bottom half, and the top half was boarded up where a window use to be. There was a six-inch slot of wood that could be opened for communication.

When I started to knock on the slot of wood, Jeanie slid open the cover and looked out the slot. Her eyes widened and she yelled, "CC! Girl, what you doin' over here?"

I told Jeanie that I'd been looking for her and wanted to make sure she was alright. She confirmed that she was, but while we were talking, the biker behind me said in a lowered voice, "Oh, that bitch is in the house." He then announced rather loudly that he was going home, and disappeared along the side of the house. Moments later, he reappeared, crouching down along the back of the house, inching toward the door. Jeanie couldn't see him through the slit in the door. With one quick side glance, the man saw me notice him, and he made the signal with his index finger to his mouth to tell me to "Shhh," and not to let on that he was coming for Jeanie.

At that moment, Jeanie broke the tension, clamoring for her manners, "Oh shoot, I'm not even thinking. Do you want to come in for a minute?" I heard her begin unlocking the door.

There was screaming inside my head, "No! Don't open the door!" but what came out of my mouth was, "No, no, that's okay. I'm going to have to go," I quickly responded. I waved off her advance, but I stared at her directly, widening my eyes as I spoke, trying to signal to her that this man was a few feet from her and was staging an attack. Playing it cool, but with a panic rising inside of me, I couldn't let the man pick up on what I was doing because I was exposed to him. I was in danger, but so was Jeanie, and she didn't pick up on my eye signals.

I heard the tumbler in the deadbolt click all the way over, and Jeanie cracked the door open. Knowing someone in the neighborhood was after her, she waved her hand for me to come in quickly, "Hurry up! Hurry up and come in."

I rushed into the kitchen at the same moment the man jumped out and rushed the door. He tackled Jeanie, both of them slamming against the cabinet. Jeanie started yelling for her son, while her attacker was yelling about money she'd stolen from him. I moved quickly to other side of the kitchen table to shield myself. A tall young man ran into the kitchen, Jeanie's son, and grabbed the biker off of his mother. In her reprieve, Jeanie picked up a white standing fan and started swinging it, bashing the biker over the back while her son held him in a headlock. Jeanie's son pushed the biker out of the back door and locked it behind him.

Jeanie, enraged, ran to the door and opened the wooden slot. "Yeah, I took your money, dumbass," she yelled out at the biker, picking himself up from the dirt yard. She went on for a bit, yelling about how stupid the man was to leave his wallet out, and the biker yelled slurs and threats back at her, promising to come back.

Jeanie closed the wooden slot, took a deep breath, turned, and greeted me with a calm voice, "So, how have you been? Come and sit down."

That's how the streets were. As chaotic as the fight was, I learned to always be hypervigilant and expect something to jump off. As the struggle was occurring I was doing my assessment. I looked at hands and bodies to see if anyone had a gun or knife. I looked around the room to see if there were any weapons out in the open. I checked the exits in case I needed to escape. I scanned the yard to see if anyone would be running in to join the fight or break it up. In those moments of assessment, I surmised that this was a house of drug addicts. No one had a gun. If they did, they would have sold it for more crack cocaine. But I did have the good sense to count my blessings and leave before Jeanie's attacker returned.

Jeanie apologized about the chaos. I hugged her, unscathed by everything that had happened, checking to make sure she was alright, then left. That was the last time I went into a crack house. From then on, if I needed to find a trapped woman who was caught up in a crack house, I sent word through someone buying or selling drugs in the house.

CHAPTER SEVENTEEN
Outlaws

There are two reasons a customer might get robbed: if there is an opportunity, and if the sex worker is an outlaw. In coming to understand the street, you realize that there are three types of street level sex work: pimp-controlled prostitution called sex trafficking, women classified as "outlaws," and those classified as "renegades."

An outlaw is someone that not only does not adhere to the traditional pimp game by not having a pimp, they are someone that is not going to engage in an honest sex-for-money exchange. Outlaws set up their customers so they can steal from them. In the world of outlaws, "Somebody's getting fucked, but nobody's having sex." An outlaw will tell you that you can have a "half-and-half" (oral sex and intercourse) for just twenty bucks, but she's likely to jump out of the car with your wallet before any sex occurs. Or she may tell a customer that sex costs twenty dollars, but will then charge them for every extra thing, like touching her breasts costs more or placing their fingers inside of her costs more, making the final cost nowhere near what was initially agreed to.

A nineteen-year-old girl named Noni, who had been abused in her home and then trafficked at fourteen years old, came to the Second Chance program. I worked with Noni for many years, even getting her a job the The Friendly Center so she could learn vocational skills. Having been trafficked into the sex trade by a pimp, Noni was savvy and so close to the streets that she knew how to eventually take advantage of the game in her own favor, becoming an outlaw by the time she was nineteen.

Noni always said, "If you got twenty bucks, then you got thirty bucks. If you got thirty bucks, maybe you got forty." Before getting out of the car, Noni would either convince the customer to give her more money or simply take it from them through sleight of hand. Simply, outlaws are mostly interested in "hitting a lick," meaning getting money quickly by robbing someone or cheating someone.

A common ploy is to first case a customer, choosing to walk up to a nice, safe looking suburban type of car, driven by a middle class man who doesn't look like he's from the neighborhood. An outlaw will approach the car when the man rolls the window down and snatch his glasses, demanding payment in exchange for their return. It's an easy twenty-dollar score. They should be prescription glasses, not sunglasses, appearing expensive to replace. It also helps if he has a wedding ring on his finger. Once this happens, the man has few choices. He can pay the twenty dollars to get his glasses back and move on, he can go home and try to make up some story about his missing glasses to his wife, he can jump out and chase the woman down an unfamiliar street or alley, or he can call the police and try to explain a very awkward situation. He's likely to cough up the money and drive away, duped. This is a simple scam that requires little-to-no effort for outlaws. Similarly, an outlaw might lure a customer around the corner for her male companion(s) to rob him at gun point.

The next rung of outlaw scheming involves a manipulation of perception. An outlaw will get into a car with a potential customer, ask what he wants to purchase, and agree on the cost. The outlaw will then flash a fake badge and tell the customer that he has just solicited an undercover cop and that he'll be arrested and taken to jail. She creates an illusion that there are other police officers waiting in the wings for her signal that he has offered her money in exchange for sex. In his panic, the customer begs not to be arrested, asking if there's anything he can do to avoid it. The outlaw offers to allow him to pay his way out of the situation, keeping his anonymity and dignity intact. She takes his cash, makes a fake signal to a random guy on the street or talks into her shirt as if she's wearing a wire, letting them know they can "stand down." The outlaw then gets out of the car and tells him not to come back or he'll be immediately apprehended. He is so thankful that he drives off penniless.

Another, more extravagant, rouse involves two people. One plays the seller and lures a customer into a house or apartment. The customer takes off his pants or sets his wallet down, occupied by the woman playing the seller. In the meantime, the other woman, who the customer doesn't know is there, steals his cash and credit cards. Sometimes, they also take his car keys and drive off in his car. The decoy excuses herself, exits, and joins her friend. They spend everything he has, and when they are done, they sell the car or leave it on the side of the road. But because outlaws are out to hit a lick, they have been known to set up other girls in the game. On occasion, when one girl thinks she's working in tandem with an outlaw to rob a customer, the outlaw will convince the girl to have sex with the customer while she sneaks in and steals his wallet. The outlaw steals as much as she can—wallet, car keys, car, and anything else—and leaves the girl having sex with the customer behind to answer for the robbery.

This is one of the reasons no one in the game has friends. They will tell you they have "associates," or people they know well, but not friends. One of my teens who often ran away from home, Gloria, was set up by an outlaw named Sarah who took Gloria under her wing to help her learn the game. This was a red flag she didn't know to look for, because no one in the game should be trusted. Gloria was sold to a pimp without her knowledge when her "friend" told Gloria she was going to hook her up with a guy that was cute and had lots of money. Together, they went to meet an African-American man in his forties who showed up in a late model Escalade. He was dressed nicely and had a pretty smile.

Sarah got in the front seat and Gloria got in the back. The two in the front seat talked quietly and low, telling Gloria they were working things out so they could have a great time all day on the man's dime. When they finished their conversation and the man handed Sarah some money, she got out of the car and told Gloria to hop up front. When Gloria moved up, Sarah told her to ride with him for a little while because he really liked her. Sarah promised she would catch up with them at a well-known local bar. Gloria agreed, feeling special that the man preferred her, when, in reality, Gloria had just been sold to a pimp.

When working with outlaws, I focus mostly on the violence that they experience and the trauma that is associated with it. Outlaws typically become outlaws as a response to the victimization they have suffered. They feel justified in robbing their customers. In some ways, outlaws have a certain type of self-esteem in that they choose to no longer be victims, but are relegated to working a system they are already entangled in. The most notorious outlaw was Aileen Wuornos, portrayed in the movie *Monster*, who killed some of her customers.

In working this way, outlaws take great risks, and they can never have repeat customers. Engaging a new customer is dangerous, so to do it for every transaction is the biggest risk of all sex trade work. With every exchange, outlaws are at high risk for serious violence. Beyond that, taking more money from a customer than he is offering is risky, and requires skill to not get caught. Making a living this way, through sex trade robbery, is a high stakes gamble, and for outlaws, it's a way of life.

It's a fact that women in prostitution who have repeat customers have safer experiences, especially as the streets are inundated with drugs. When outlaws get high and become addicted, they get in and out of cars without remembering faces, and risk interacting with someone they've cheated or stolen from. Some women get back into the car of someone they've stolen from only to be beaten by him. But like Noni, instead of being victimized, outlaws believe they're choosing to be the victimizer, thereby taking some of the power back by—in Noni' words, "Getting them before they get me." These women choose to be the predator instead of the prey. For most women that have been trafficked and then continue to stay in the sex trade, traumatization is a common experience. Trauma occurs repeatedly, causing women to suffer "complex trauma," and outlaws have suffered greatly and choose to hurt others. It's important to assess an outlaw's criminal mindset, and to help them be safe, feel safe, meet their basic needs, and attend to their complex trauma.

CHAPTER EIGHTEEN
Renegades

Renegades are similar to outlaws in that they choose not to follow tradition. They work independent of a pimp, earning them the title "renegades," as opposed to the natural order of things. However, unlike outlaws, renegades do adhere to the rules of the work. They will engage in sex-for-money exchanges with customers for an agreed upon price, earning every dollar they make through hard work on their back. Just like outlaws, renegades are adult women. Youth involved in the sex trade are automatically victims of the crime of sex trafficking if they are involved in the commercial sex trade. Sex traffickers often try to "pull" renegades, meaning recruit them, attempting to put them under their control, which can be tempting because it's quite dangerous for renegades out on the street. This may involve anything from sweet-talking women to strong arm tactics with the threat or presence of violence.

Without protection, renegades face the wrath of sex traffickers while they are out on the street. Being that renegades are taking up space and money where traffickers have working girls, renegades have to be careful to watch for them. Being a renegade, Toni faced this situation in the north end quite often. One pimp would try and beat her up when he saw her to discourage her from working in his territory and to, instead, work for him. He would remind her by telling her after a beating, "And bitch, every time I see you, this is what's going to happen."

Not only do renegades have to be careful in terms of watching out for sex traffickers, they also have little protection from customers. They don't have any recourse from physical violence, protection from customers that want a relationship instead of a sex-for-money exchange, or protection from sexually transmitted infections, including HIV. Renegades engage in elaborate measures to counter these risks, like the chatting and checking ritual and choosing a comfortable date spot where the transaction can take place, decreasing the potential for violence. In the same way that outlaws buck the system to be independent, so do renegades. But while outlaws trick customers out of a psychological need for a type of revenge, renegades pride themselves on being entrepreneurial sex workers, despite the grave risk involved.

Oral sex is the most common form of sex purchased on the street, and because renegades don't have anyone protecting them, they have to make many tactical and strategic decisions during a transaction. Once they arrive at the date spot, the seller will carefully choreograph the oral sex experience with her safety in mind. From the passenger side of the car, she will place her left foot close to the center of the floor, taking a strong stance. She keeps her right foot near the door so that, in the event that she needs to jump out of the car in a hurry, she can push off from her left foot while at the same time stepping out with the right foot. Her right hand will either be around his penis to stop him from pushing her head down and gagging her, or it will be close to the car door handle, allowing her to open the car door quickly. Her left hand will likely rest on his shoulder so that she can easily punch him if needed. To make a quick and seamless escape, she would punch him with her left fist, open the car door with her right hand, push off with her left foot, and step out with her right foot, making a quick exit. In other words, all of her moves during a sexual transaction, whether it is oral sex or intercourse, are thought out and choreographed for her safety.

For her safety, on occasion, Toni has hired friends to watch her and make sure she returns unharmed. Typically, these "watchers" are people in the neighborhood, hanging out, or young people riding bikes up and down the street. She will give them ten dollars to make sure they write down the make and model of the car she got in and to make sure they watch for her return. If she works a bar, she may pay someone to recruit customers, send them her way, then watch as she leaves and returns. She may give a friend ten dollars for every customer in the bar they send over to her that results in a sex-for-money exchange.

For prevention against sexually transmitted infections, and because some customers do not want to use a condom, many women have learned to be savvy. Demanding or negotiating condom use has lost women potential money as a customer will go to the next woman. To protect against HIV and other sexually transmitted diseases, some women will agree not to use a condom and then, at the date spot, slip the condom on and off of the customer without his knowledge. Toni explained to me that she would place the condom in her mouth and keep it on the side of her cheek.

"If it's oral sex, you put your mouth on him and put the tip of the condom on the tip of his penis. You use your hand wrapped around his penis to slowly roll the condom down onto his penis while you are giving him head." After the customer ejaculates, the seller uses her hand to roll the condom up and off of the penis. "He never knew he wore a condom," Toni says, making hand motions throughout her explanation.

For protection during intercourse, Toni explained a more elaborate scheme in which the woman must be in charge of guiding the penis into the vagina, at which point she slides the condom on him. At the conclusion, she grabs his penis as he backs out of her vagina to hold the condom so that he backs out of the condom as well.

With freedom from a trafficker as a renegade comes the ability to take on varying specialty clients. Though these dates pose different threats, they can be very lucrative. Toni has made some of her money from customers that want something other than the usual oral, vaginal, and anal sex. On occasion, she has had customers that want to tie her up with duct tape and play out rape fantasies. One customer regularly put duct tape over her mouth, around her wrists, and around her ankles, and then would rub himself against her until ejaculation. Another regular customer paid her to put three razor blades in between her four fingers and masturbate him, creating small droplets of blood from his penis. If she cut him too deep, she would have to pay the physical consequences. Toni also had a regular customer who she dropped everything for whenever he was in town. He was a business man, and the date always started and ended the same way. They would stop at the local pharmacy and pick up a box of Ex-Lax. She would take some, and then he would take her out to a big dinner, where they would talk about his work and his travels. He would take her back to a condo he rented—it was always the same place—where he'd put on music for them. The condo had a glass dining table that Toni would dance on top of for the man. He laid under the glass table and masturbated while she removed her underwear and defecated on the table for him to see. This would bring him to climax. This was a $500 date. Mary and other renegades most often preferred these specialty dates. Despite the psychological trauma associated with their oddities, they caused no physical trauma to the body, which the women preferred.

When working with renegades, as with all of my clients, I was most concerned with the violence they faced, the psychological trauma, their emotional and mental health, and particularly with their risk for sexually transmitted infections. I worry about sexually transmitted infections in renegades more so than in outlaw women because outlaws are the least likely to actually be having any sexual contact.

While renegades and outlaws feel like they're getting the upper hand because they're not pimp controlled, they're still just victims in wolves clothing. They're still women who are being physically, emotionally, and psychologically tormented day-in and day-out; caught in the vicious cycle of sex trade and drug addiction. And worst of all, they're all likely there because they were once controlled by a trafficker—maybe even someone they knew, that they were close with. These are the women and girls that society has turned a blind eye to, have thrown away. And being an outreach worker, especially at the start, means knowing that you can only institute change on the smallest of scales, inch by inch, and while I was deep in this world, starting to finally make real and tangible breakthroughs, I would be faced with my biggest heartbreak yet.

CHAPTER NINETEEN
Sex-Trafficked Youth

The youngest girl I've ever interacted with was twelve. She was a part of a federal sting that rescued over twenty girls from Toledo being forced to work a truck stop in Harrisburg, Pennsylvania in 2005. When I first met her, my thought was, "How does a community lose twenty girls and no one really notices?" That thought infuriated me. There were no sirens. The news stations weren't breaking in with special reports. There was no community outrage. The recovery of these girls fell silent, and deep down, I knew why there was no outrage. It was because of who they were and where they came from. They were children of poor people. People with no voice. These children didn't matter. Each one had likely been deemed a runaway, and we don't do anything more for poor girls of color who run away than wait for them to run back. There was no intervention. Police departments engage in passive enforcement when runaways are concerned, so calling them runaways gave them an excuse to forego an active investigation.

If you can, picture the face and body of a twelve-year-old girl. I'm looking in the face of a child that is not even fully developed, stumbling over my words, trying to figure out how we are going to have a conversation about her experiences and where we go from here. If there is evil in the world, what was done to Rebecca is it. Her abusers were not kind. They didn't take into consideration that she was twelve and scared out of her mind. She's a prostitute. In her customer's minds, she's used to this type of treatment. As we talked, I thought about how few words she actually knew to express herself. Rebecca had a very limited vocabulary, and she was very shy and timid. I ended up linking her with one of the best social workers in the field and in my community to help her.

There isn't a Code Adam when you're a teenager. There isn't an Amber Alert. Nothing scrolls across your television screen when a teen runs away. There are no alerts that appear on your phone. If you are thirteen years old or younger, police will actually look for you. But when a young person is older than fourteen, there isn't really an effort to search for them. Police departments haven't caught up with the fact that being a runaway is the number one risk factor for sex trafficking.

All too often in situations like this, a missing teen's mother calls the police, and the police enter the conversation under the assumption that the child ran away. The officer will start asking questions to build the argument, like: Did you have an argument? Have you ever had an argument and your child ran off or stayed out over night? When was the last time they ran away? These are all very reasonable questions, but it becomes a problem when an officer refuses to entertain any other theory, including the one that perhaps the child ran away and is currently being sold by traffickers. The search for these "endangered runaways" often doesn't go further than an officer stopping and questioning some kids on the street corner, asking them if they have identification.

A runaway is considered a low-level incident. And if, or when, the youth is recovered and had been a runaway, officers aren't required to do a post recovery interview to ask the youth about where they had been and how they have been able to survive. Where did they sleep? How did they get money? Did they trade sex to survive or were they sexually exploited? These are critical questions that may lead officers to unmask sexual exploitation, as runaways may find themselves desperate. They may be taken advantage and manipulated into sexual encounters in exchange for a place to stay, food to eat, drugs, clothes, and other basic needs.

In Rebecca's case, she had been trafficked on her own block at home. When she arrived in Harrisburg, she discovered another little girl there from her neighborhood. She was forced to service men at a truck stop. Her "bottom," the woman that serves as, for lack of a better word, assistant manager for the organization, walked her to truck after truck. Her bottom wanted to get in each truck with her to watch the interaction. The bottom's job was to train her well, make sure she didn't have conversations with a truck driver to encourage him to help her escape, and to make sure all of the money was handed over. Rebecca was found by law enforcement during a sting and returned to Toledo.

The recovery of the twelve-year-old young white girl was reported in the paper, with the headline eluding to a twelve-year-old prostitute being rescued. The media called this victim of a crime a "prostitute," retraumatizing an already traumatized child. As a result, Rebecca was horribly teased at school. The school exercised a severe lack of discretion in helping her to acclimate back into the school system, nor did they prepare her peers. Nothing was done. This girl, who already suffered learning disabilities and a great deal of emotional and psychological damage, became the target of bullies and was forced out of her school. A colleague of mine, Linda, agreed to work with Rebecca.

Linda worked closely with this young child over the next several years, helping her to find counseling, housing, and a listening ear whenever she needed it. By their third year of work together, Linda closed the case because Rebecca had been doing as well as could be expected and there were others to tend to. Even though Rebecca was set on a stable path toward success, we knew that the damage ran deep. Rebecca stopped contacting Linda, slipped into depression, and the next time I heard about her, Linda called to say Rebecca overdosed on heroin at just eighteen years old.

During this time in my life, I interacted with many trafficked teens. Most of the women I'd worked with previously were first trafficked by a pimp or molested over and over by a family member or friend of the family. Now, I was regularly getting to the kids before they reached eighteen. In 2008, I chose to do in-depth interviews with fourteen of them in one year. There were two things that struck me from those in-depth interviews. One was that each time I was driving home after the interview, I tried to think of things I would have done differently if I were given the same set of circumstances that each young person was given. And even though I could think of different ways to handle situations they described, I couldn't come up with a "better" response than what they did. I wouldn't have made a different choice given the same set of circumstances. I also found out that each one of those children wanted a normal life and a family that loved them. They wanted to meet the love of their life and buy a home and be happy. They wanted very traditional lives, but because of circumstance, they ended up living their lives trying to survive instead of thrive.

I consistently asked each one of them to tell me the most important message they thought adults should know about how to help kids like them. One very wise young person said to tell the adults "to talk about it." In many colorful words, she explained that when we talk about it as adults, we give youth the permission to talk about it. Another young person said, "Keep us busy and positive." This young person tapped into what we all try to do as parents. We pay for our children to be on the softball team, the volleyball team, to go to computer camp, and to be a cheerleader. We spend our time doing these things, not necessarily because we think our child will earn a sports scholarship, but because we all know one universal truth: if we keep our children busy and positive, that maybe when we turn out the light at night, they go to sleep instead of sneaking out of the house to get into trouble.

Finally, another collection of comments centered around keeping kids safe and preventing them from being trafficked, as opposed to the current model, which is to wait for them to be trafficked and then rush to do something about it. And, indeed, it is our resposibility as adults to keep kids safe. It's our responsibility to pass laws and to be aware of the dangers out there, and to put protections in place that keep kids safe. Unfortunately, we continue to fail them.

CHAPTER TWENTY

Sex Traffickers

Sex traffickers are pimps and pimps are sex traffickers. The name changed so that the world would come to understand the seriousness of the crime. The word "pimp" has been taken over by pop culture and is a word that young people use in a way that does not signify the exploitation of someone. Whatever your personal feelings are about the takeover of the word, when pop culture uses the word, they have left out the components violence and exploitation, only adopting the power associated with the word. The word "pimp" is a caricature of its former self, signifying coolness in its user, but not abuse. Someone may answer the phone, "Pimping," instead of, "Hello." It doesn't mean they are involved in the business of sex trafficking, but that they are handling their business with the swagger and power of a pimp.

Trafficking is the word that signifies the systematic exploitation and enslavement of another human being for the economic profit of others. I use the words "pimp" and "trafficker" interchangeably because, although society uses the term trafficker, those involved in the real game of trafficking still refer to real pimps as pimps.

The world of sex trafficking is a complex network of rules, players, and survival—more so than most people realize—making it nearly impossible for victims to escape. Human trafficking is modern day slavery and slavery is as old as time itself. Human trafficking in the U.S. consists of both labor and sex trafficking of victims born within the U.S. border as well as those brought into the country. What I'm most familiar with is the manifestation of slavery through the lens of street-based prostitution and the sex trafficking of U.S. children.

In looking through this lens exclusively, pimps may be male or female, although pimping is still largely a male dominated field. Although types of and levels of pimps are not mutually exclusive and they often overlap, I present them here as discrete entities for clarity's sake.

Tennis shoe pimps are the lowest rung of pimp on the ladder and are least respected in the pimping world. They are not professional players, and in the real underground game, they wouldn't even be considered a pimp. However, he is a pimp in the eyes of the law if he has convinced someone to sell sex for money and give it to him. Tennis shoe pimps are usually poor or drug addicted men who have convinced someone to sell sex for money or drugs or to pay the rent. I've met one couple where the male heterosexual partner also sold sex to men, but it is most often the female in the relationship that will sell sex to afford the couple the things they need. The male doesn't have other women that he controls and doesn't really consider himself a pimp or to be in the pimping business. However, under the law, if he is forcing or coercing her, or if she is underage and she is giving him the money, he is considered a trafficker. Most often, law enforcement is not much interested in this type of pimp.

Some drug dealers may engage in pimping activities, particularly if they have a trap house (the name "crack house" changed to "trap house" when other drugs became popular) or a clientele of drug-addicted women. These dope boys focus primarily on drug sales, and if there is some money to be made in prostitution then they may indulge, but their main products are likely popular street drugs. Trap house pimps allow a drug-addicted woman or two to stay at the trap house, but the women may also be held in sexual servitude to the men there. Again, this person serving in the pimp role is not understood to be a pimp in the underground economy, but is technically serving in the role of a trafficker as he is taking his victim's freedom and selling or providing her to his "boys" or associates. Most times, she stays in the trap house because he is consistently feeding her drugs and her addiction won't allow her to leave. Sometimes she stays because he is holding her there. The opposite is also true. Some dope boys will move into a woman's house, begin selling drugs, take over paying the rent and eventually all of the bills. A woman may agree to these terms initially, but over time, if she presents a problem, the dealer will start feeding her drugs for free. Eventually, he will start making her pay for the drugs until she has nothing to pay except for the trade of her body.

Next, a guerilla pimp is a professional player pimp who is known to be ruthless. He uses violence, or guerilla techniques, to recruit and control his victims. Even though guerilla pimps are considered professional player pimps, they are not as respected as a finesse pimp. Guerilla pimps are brash and violent, never taking the time to groom their victims. In one case I was a part of, two girls, fourteen and fifteen years old, were walking to Wendy's to get Frostys when they were stopped by a man and woman in a vehicle. The man convinced them he was one their friend's father, and the presence of the woman helped the girls to trust him. He asked if they wanted a ride to Wendy's. When the girls accepted and got in the car, he took them to his house where he threatened, intimidated, and became physically violent with them until they submitted to his demand to work as prostitutes.

Guerilla pimping doesn't make much business sense in the underground world of sex trafficking, and so it's not as popular. Since trafficking is seen by pimps as a business, it is in the best interest of pimps to look for opportunities where they can make money off of their victims for a very long time. In the wake of the human trafficking movement, snatching kids off of the street just doesn't make good business sense anymore. When a fourteen and fifteen-year-old are snatched in my community, they are each a "hot kid," and it's likely that parents and advocates will stress to the police the need for an active investigation. It will be difficult to sell them for a long period of time, because getting caught with them could mean significant time in prison. This translates into taking a high amount of risk for a temporary or low gain. The money to be made just isn't worth the risk. And that's why it's not popular, despite the myriad of television shows, news reports, and photos showing girls in chains. The media only showcases the most sensationalized version of trafficking.

Finesse pimps are the most popular type of professional player pimp. Instead of brute force, they use their intelligence, charismatic personality, skills, and talents to finesse vulnerable women and youth into their lair. A finesse pimp is someone that typically has been mentored by an older pimp, or O.G. pimp (a.k.a. original gangster pimp), that has been in the game for a while. The first and most important lesson that a pimp learns is how to perceive the world and men's place in it. He is the king and has the power to manipulate the world and those in it. He will teach him that perspective is everything. Not only does he have to have a solid perception of himself as a pimp and his place on his throne, but he has to consistently convey this to the victims he has in his stable.

The O.G. pimp will teach him the rules of the game—how he should dress, think, and behave, how he should approach women, who he should approach and not approach and why, what he should say, and how he should finesse them. He will teach him how to build an entourage and the roles each member should play.

A successful professional pimp knows people. This is his talent. He typically has impeccable assessment skills, and he understands his victim's deepest desires, disappointments, and especially her vulnerabilities. He learns what these vulnerabilities are so he can exploit them.

Successful finesse pimps have good emotional intelligence and they are charismatic. They use their personality and assessment skills in tandem to convince girls to sell sex for them. When a mother approaches me to tell me that she thinks her daughter is being approached by a sex trafficker, I immediately know one thing: he thinks her daughter is vulnerable, and she probably is. I tell the mother to involve the criminal justice system if she can, but most importantly, to respond to the vulnerability inside her daughter. I tell her to do everything she possibly can, but the best thing is to use all her energy and strength to fill the vulnerability in her child. The criminal justice system may not be able to deter the trafficker, particularly if he has a willing victim, but filling the vulnerability will make him walk away freely. He will no longer be interested.

I don't want to portray finesse pimps as nonviolent lover-boys, because they certainly are not. They use whatever skill they have that is most appropriate for the time. They use their charisma when they have to, and they use extreme physical violence when they feel it is necessary. They are usually not violent psychopaths, however, they use violence as a method of control. They are as dangerous, if not more than, a guerilla pimp, because a finesse pimp is in it for the long haul. He will manipulate, control, and sell his victims for as long as he possibly can. He will ride his horse until it drops or until he has gotten every penny out of it. He will tell her what she needs to hear to keep her in her place and doing exactly what he wants her to do. He knows that controlling the mind through love and fear is stronger than controlling the body with chains. He will tell her that he loves her. He will ask for her love and devotion to him. She will need to tell him everything she is thinking and feeling so that he can control what she thinks and feels. He is so deep into her mind that if she has to go to the bathroom, she might consider asking him how many squares of toilet paper to use because, without his advice, she really isn't quite sure. He convinces her that love and devotion means he should enter her every thought.

R. Kelly is a prime example of a finesse pimp's technique. Although R. Kelly has never been accused of selling girls, he uses the exact techniques that a pimp uses to manipulate and control. He is incredibly charming, successful, and each girl believed he could help them access the music business. Naïve parents turned their children over to him, believing he would mentor them and nurture their budding singing careers.

Robert Kelly began by being each girl's closest friend, mentor, and confidant. He got into their heads and asked each to rely on him, promising to provide everything they needed. As each began to rely on him, he moved from mentorship into sexual relationships with them, and these young, impressionable girls fell in love with such a charismatic and powerful man. Soon they had to inform him of everywhere they went, including the bathroom. They had to ask to eat and get his permission for every move, including when they could call their parents and what they would say. He harbored more than one girl in his house and had an ongoing sexual relationship with them all. Most of the girls reported they were there voluntarily and didn't want to leave. However, he is nearby every time they report that everything is fine and that they love him. The parents, who know their children best, stand confused. As they watch their children turn eighteen and stay locked away with this man, they know something is dreadfully wrong but are hopeless in their attempts to get their daughters back.

The untrained eye simply sees teens having sex with an older, charismatic celebrity. Some people see fast little girls who wanted to have sex with a powerful man to advance their careers. Sometimes, African-American's see white America trying to take another successful black man down in these cases, and racism helps white Americans see another person of color as a predator and a criminal. But all of these perceptions are functioning under the guise of a sex trafficker who has warped and brainwashed the minds of his victims.

Finesse pimps create and capitulate Stockholm syndrome and trauma bonding. They target and manipulate the training we've already given to all of our little girls. We sit them in front of the television as babies and turn on the "classics"—Cinderella, Beauty and the Beast, The Little Mermaid, Sleeping Beauty—and we inadvertently warp their value as young women. They learn that Cinderella could never be happy until she married a man. They learn that Sleeping Beauty was doomed to be paralyzed, comatose, until a man kissed her. Both of these women had virtually no happiness in their lives until men made them whole. The Little Mermaid taught girls that it's alright to give up your home and your voice if it's for a man. And after Belle enters Beast's castle to take the place of her imprisoned father, then becoming the prisoner, falls in love with Beast, her captor. Plus, falling in love with a beast and trying to change or "save" him is a story told over and over in domestic violence courts and in trafficking cases. Victims convince themselves, under the thumb of their trafficker, that their love for him is strong enough to stop him from abusing her—that one day they'll be together, forever. Stockholm syndrome. Trauma bonding.

Stockholm syndome and trauma bonding is a common experience, and happens when someone spends time with a person who isolates and controls them. It happens when one person in a relationship holds all of the power and controls the thoughts, opinions, and perspectives of their partner. Over time, victims begin to develop a strong psychological alliance with their captor. The psyche does this subconsciously as a means of survival. When someone has power, isolation, and control over someone's thoughts, behavior, and feelings, the psyche not only begins to believe everything their captor is saying, they begin to identify with them. Subconsciously, the mind and body do this for survival reasons, knowing that if their captor is happy and satisfied, the more likely it is that they keep breathing, eating, and are less likely to suffer physical or psychological pain. Loyalty and bonding are common defense mechanisms when survival is at stake.

If a pimp's victim needs to dream that one day they will be together, then he will plant those thoughts in her mind very sweetly. He will demand complete loyalty. Their success will be won on her back, and the harder she works, the faster they can realize their success. He will let her know that the way he looks, what he wears, and what he drives is a measure of her hard work or lack thereof. If he is walking around in less than the best, it is because she has failed as a partner. If possible, he will wear designer clothes, designer shoes, and designer jackets. His hair will be cut and edged. He will look and smell his best at all times, because his body and his conversation are the tools he uses in his job. His contribution to this partnership is to love her, protect her, and cultivate the vision for where they are going in life. Her contribution is to work hard and give him her money because he controls the master plan, thinking strategically for the both of them.

A successful pimp wants women to see that he has other girls or women. He wants each to see that another girl may be prettier, harder working, and more loyal. He uses this to motivate each to work harder.

When we think of the traditional pimp of the seventies, we think of him wearing a loud purple suit with a pimped-out hat, complete with a feather sticking out of it. But if any pimp is going to wear the traditional pimp dress, it will be a "mack." Occasionally and depending on the event, a mack might wear the traditional outfit and be clean from head to toe. His outfit, his hair, his shoes, and his jewelry, will all be expensive and exquisite.

Macks are player pimps at the highest levels. To provide an illustration, in Las Vegas, tourists and vacationers play the slots, cards, and take in a few shows. They are akin to tennis shoe pimps. They're not really into gambling and wouldn't be gambling if they weren't in Vegas, having fun. Then there are the serious gamblers. These people are akin to player pimps. They gamble regularly, and they go to Las Vegas specifically to spend their time gambling. They are not interested in going to the shows. Much like the player pimps whose eyes are on pimping, serious gambler's eyes are solely on gambling, and they spend a considerable amount of time and money engaging in gambling. The casino wants to keep them coming back, so they provide them with comps that allow them to get rooms cheaply or to stay a few nights for free. They provide them with meals and other luxuries that keep them coming back. Then there are what the casino refers to as "whales." Whales are the few gamblers who come to Vegas to spend a massive amount of money. Casinos may send a private jet to pick up a whale. They may provide this person with a luxury suite, the best food, and even male or female companionship. Whales are comparable to macks in the pimping business. Macks are well known in the business, established, respected, at the top of the hierarchy, and they may be national or international players. Some former rappers claim they have been pimps, namely Snoop Dog, whose current nickname is "Mack," and who was allegedly a pimp from 2003 to 2004. Another well-known rap artist turned actor, Ice-T, was reportedly a pimp for a very short while.

As a professional player pimp will tell you, to respect the game and become a professional player takes skill. Ice-T says it's like "trying to teach astrophysics to a third grader." There are many rules and lessons to becoming a professional pimp. Once inducted into the game, professional player pimps establish finite rules that must be followed. They understand that if their women become drug addicted that they will lose any and all power they have over them, because no matter how much she loves and fears him, she will not remain loyal and will end up giving all of her money to dope boys instead of him. Therefore, a sex trafficker may allow their women to use drugs as a reward, or to help make the job easier, but professional pimps regulate the frequency and the type of drugs they allow the girls to use. For instance, smoking marijuana is not a problem and, in fact, is not even considered a drug on the street. Likewise, powder cocaine, MDMA, and other similar drugs are not frowned upon.

However, during the nineties, in the height of the crack cocaine epidemic, most professional pimps did not allow their women to use crack cocaine. Crack cocaine is bad for business in that women who smoke it and become addicted are consumed with getting more crack cocaine instead of working for their pimp. Because a crack high only lasts a few minutes, girls were trying to jump in and out of cars as quickly as possible so they could get back to their drug dealer to buy more crack cocaine. Over time, a drug-addicted woman is no longer interested in giving her pimp the money. She is most interested in giving her money to the dope boy. In addition, crack cocaine is not a social drug, so women who use prefer to squirrel themselves away to smoke all day. In the event that the pimp was also the drug dealer, he would have to be in constant contact with his victim, supplying drugs to her and collecting money. As crack cocaine abusers, women lost interest in their appearance and in their job performance, only doing enough to feed their habit. Customers would report they preferred commercial sex BC, or "before crack."

The introduction of crack cocaine in the eighties and nineties drove more women into street-based prostitution and left pimps out of the equation. Women quickly learned that once they'd sold everything for the drug, the only thing they had left to sell was their bodies. This new generation of prostitutes was so apparent that advocates and researchers in the nineties often wrote about crack cocaine becoming the new pimp.

However, in recent times, crack cocaine has been largely replaced by the explosion of prescription opiates and heroin. Pimps quickly came to understand that the heroin high lasts longer, and that women who are high on heroin are more docile and much more likely to sell sexual services for the pimp. Because heroin brought more middle class girls and white women into the trade, traffickers had ample opportunities to exploit them while also continuing to exploit low income, high risk girls and women. Of course, women on heroin with few resources left are vulnerable enough to sell themselves to customers who will pay them for sex, independent of a pimp.

The pimp in control of heroin-addicted girls and women will divide the amount she uses per day by her potential to earn, and uses this incremental dosing formula as a way to control her. He will set a quota she must earn to make him a profit. Conversely, other professional sex traffickers will not allow their women to do heroin or any other drug that comes with overwhelmingly addictive qualities, such as crack cocaine or crystal meth.

It's all about the game, and a victim's devotion to her pimp must be complete and authentic, not harried by drug addiction. She will continue to work until he says stop, and he will never say stop. As Ice-T notes, "A pimp is going to work you until you burned down, busted, or dead." In Iceberg Slim's book, *Pimp*, a book that every professional pimp reads, he discusses the concept of "mileage on a ho," meaning the length of time a pimp can sell a victim before she gives out. And because he is everything to his women, pimps typically have their girls and women call them "Daddy," because they structure their practice in such a way that their victims believe they are providing everything for them as well as meeting all of their emotional and physical needs. A victim may even be made to tattoo proof of his ownership on her body.

If any of the rules are broken by a victim, they are deemed "out of pocket," meaning the girl is engaging in behavior that costs, or has the potential to cost, the pimp money. These violations might include not bringing in the quota, not dressing appropriately for the job, being too high for the job, or talking back, among a number of other infractions. This is a dangerous position for any girl to be in because victims are subject to be "broke," meaning they will suffer the consequence designed to break a victim's spirit and bring about total submission. Whatever the violation, money or the potential loss of money is at stake. The response may or may not be physically violent, but it is always extremely psychologically intimidating. In a pimp's world, a victim that is out of pocket needs to learn quickly to never put his money at risk again.

The whole street game is analogous to equestrianism. A successful professional pimp has a "stable" of women and youth. He puts them out on the "track" to make him money. When someone catches a wild horse, the first thing they do is to "break" her so that she fully submits to the new owner and does their bidding.

Once they are broken, a pimp sets a quota that each victim must bring in each night they work. Two trafficked teens who admitted to me they hated selling sex, but were afraid of not coming back without having made their quota, sold their clothes, their friends' clothes, jumped and robbed people, and started stealing from stores so they could return the items for cash in hopes of meeting their quota each night. Only when they couldn't make enough money did they have sex for money.

For most pimps, a victim talking to another pimp is an out of pocket offense. It's a serious violation, and girls are not allowed to talk to another pimp unless they are "choosing up." If she chooses up, that means she is choosing this new pimp. Otherwise, there is no need for conversation between the two. Because victims learn to manipulate men sexually for a living, pimps cannot allow their victims to begin to sexually manipulate them by providing conversation to different pimps. If that happens, and she begins to talk to her pimp and other pimps, then, over time, she might manipulate them, "get inside their head" and invert the power structure. To prevent this, the unanimous pimp's code does not allow for this type of behavior.

Similarly, pimps refer to "reckless eyeballing," or the act of giving eye contact to another pimp. Some pimps won't even allow their women to give extended eye contact to a drug dealer or young male who that pimp thinks might be getting in the game. Around other players, girls are to keep their eyes pointed to the floor. Too much eye contact with another pimp may signal that she is thinking of manipulating him or choosing him.

I've met a few professional player pimps, but I've never met a mack. They are rare, and it's difficult to get in their company unless you travel in their circles. The few professional player pimps I've known included some who were imprisoned for trafficking and decided to change their lives.

Pimps are interesting characters in that they have incredible egos. I've met few pimps that didn't want to brag about their accomplishments in some form or fashion and then write a book about it. They are incredibly charming and very likeable until you remember the way they use and abuse victims. Pimps, regardless of their lack of morality and the ethically disparaging nature of their work, aspire to be high achievers, and successful pimps are very intelligent.

A particularly well-known pimp who was also a high profile public personality agreed to be interviewed by me. After our interview, he asked if I wanted to see his cathouse. I certainly did. For a researcher, the opportunity for this type of observation and immersion is very compelling, and helps me to develop better, more poignant strategies for outreach and interventions. As expected, he was also an intriguing guy. He was charming and good looking, of course, and very polite. Having received an education both on the street and in the classroom, I knew that he would be charismatic, charming, and inviting. I also knew that if I entered his cathouse with him alone that he could very easily flip the script, change, and become vicious and very dangerous. When he smiled and asked, "Would you like to see the house and the set up?" I looked into his eyes, knowing he would never tell me anything about his real intentions.

I had to keep my body language calm and cool, not revealing to him my true intentions in any way. To give myself more time to think, I quickly asked, "Where is it?" In my mind, I was rapidly cataloguing who I'd told that I would be talking to him today in case I did decide to go and see the "set up." I realized that I hadn't told anybody. I was disappointed in myself. I wanted to see the house, the inner workings of it all, but the situation wasn't as safe as I wanted it to be. I argued with myself for a few moments before realizing that although I wished the circumstances were a bit different, that this opportunity was both rare and crucial to my work. Quickly, I blurted, "Yes, I want to see it. I'll meet you over there."

When I made this decision, I banked on getting back in my car to drive there, and then I could call someone to tell them what I was doing, but to my dismay, he gestured with his hand and said, "It's just around the corner," waiting for me to start walking.

With poise, I delivered a quick excuse, "Well, I'm not going to leave my car here in this raggedy neighborhood. It might get broken into."

The man said, "Okay," and headed around the corner. I went to my car and called my mother to tell her what I was about to do and how long I should be.

"If I don't call you back in twenty minutes, send the police," I instructed and gave her the address.

The house fit right into the north Toledo neighborhood it sat in. Nothing in particular stood out about the house. It looked like the regular home of a working class family. I walked into what I imagined was once the living room, and I stood there, stoic, waiting to see if he might grab me and ask if I was the police or some other sort of imposter. When that didn't happen right away, I breathed a sigh of relief, but kept my guard up in case he was waiting to strike. The living room was furnished with a circular couch, a few chairs, and a bar. There was a large stereo system hooked up, and the bar was fully stocked with every type of liquor I could think of. The place looked like a typical after hours spot, a few of which existed in the north end, the only difference was that there were 8x10 pictures of about six women hanging on the wall behind the bar. They were scantily clothed, and he pointed out that these were the women he had in his stable. He then asked if I wanted to go upstairs and see the bedrooms, to which I declined, thanked him, and politely excused myself.

As I drove off, I called my mother back and told her I was okay, to which she scorned, "Why do you do this?" I told her that girls die and no one cares, that someone has to try and do something about it—that the more I learn, the better I can help.

As I continued to drive, I started to get scared. I started worrying that he'd shared too much information with me, and I prayed that he didn't get raided any time soon so that he wouldn't connect his bust to what he'd told and showed me, thinking that I told the police.

I have been in the company of a few pimps since then who were released from prison. One former trafficker that I didn't know sent his daughter to meet with me. She was one of the students in our social work program at the University of Toledo, pursuing her bachelor's degree. She was a very bright girl, well put together and studious. As she introduced herself and began talking, I couldn't help but think that she must be around twenty years old, which meant she likely lost her father to prison for trafficking around twelve years old. I thought about how she must have felt growing up through some of her formative years without her father, and how much of a woman warrior she was to pursue her degree.

While once holding a sex trafficking awareness event at the local mall, we had a table where social work interns handed out materials about human trafficking to teens and to their parents. As part of our event at the mall, we showed a primetime special called "Kidnapped Cousins" in the mall's theater. It was about two teenagers who were trafficked in Toledo. The plan was to show the film, then turn up the lights so I could talk a little about sex trafficking and take questions from the audience. It wasn't a successful venture. We only had about twenty-five people show up, but I wanted to greet everyone walking into the theater before the documentary started, so I was standing on the ramp, and as people opened the door and made their way into the theater to sit down, I thanked them for coming.

As I was thanking people, a guy walked passed me to take his seat. I had never met him, but when he walked past, I got a very strange feeling and I turned to watch him as he took his seat. He was thin with long, hanging dreadlocks. I thought he resembled the mugshot of the trafficker who would appear in the film, but the man in the film had short hair and a lot more weight on him. I continued to stare at this man as he took his seat and the movie began.

Even though we had security in the theater, I decided to walk over and sit down next to him. I was pretty sure it was him, and I introduced myself as I reached my hand out to shake his. He returned the handshake, but instead of announcing his name, he just said responded with, "Nice to meet you." I learned later that security also spotted this former trafficker and had their eye on me the whole time, and would have greatly preferred that I had not taken matters into my own hands. But I had forgotten about security, and was used to handling situations as best I could myself.

Throughout the movie, I was attempting to gauge whether he was agitated or angry. I needed to understand his mood so that if there was the potential for violence I would have time to notify security before anyone could be hurt. I engaged him in some small talk, and he didn't seem agitated at all. At the end of the film, the lights came up and I started to hold a conversation about domestic minor sex trafficking when he stood up and announced to the audience that he was, indeed, the trafficker in the film.

The audience gasped and waited for me or him to say or do something. Being a social worker for many years, I have become trained to see and hear very disturbing information, but have learned to maintain a poker face and not react. I thanked him for coming and asked him if he was open to questions and discussion. Once he confirmed that he was, the audience asked him a lot of questions about the incident, about his time in prison, and about his perspective. He was charming and well-spoken, as many finesse pimps are. After the theater, I met up with him several times and learned more about his background. He made the choice to be a predator, and for that, he served several years in prison. After he paid his debt to society and was freed, he had an interest in returning to school, hoping to transfer some previous college credits he carried.

Our work together focused on helping him return to school and finish his degree. The more opportunities he had to find a job that offered a living wage, the less of a chance he would think about returning to victimizing others. Unfortunately, as smart as he was, he was unable to finish school. Similar to his victims, he, too, suffered trauma from prison. Some of the buildings he had to walk through to his classes were made of cinder block. The narrow halls to class reminded him of prison and, although subtle, his heart would race with the anxiety and stress of being locked away. He couldn't bring himself to walk through those hallways and be reminded of having his freedom taken away. Instead, he ended up connecting with a friend of mine who helps men transition out of prison find jobs in the community.

The most difficult but important part of being a social worker is understanding and applying your knowledge of the cycle of abuse. All too often, abusers were once victims of abuse in some way. We learn abusive behaviors. They aren't inherent. So although traffickers are committing heinous crimes that I've dedicated my life to stopping, I also understand that these perpetrators need help out of their own cycles of abuse, that they need rehabilitation so they can potentially infiltrate the same systems they've come from to effect positive and lasting change. Hurt people hurt people, but healed people heal people, so when I have the opportunity to lend my skills to the rehabilitation of a perpetrator, I don't turn away or scoff at them in disgust. I take hold of that opportunity as part of my job to fight abuse in the streets.

CHAPTER TWENTY-ONE
The Business of Sex

In the sex trafficking business, the trafficker plays a large role, but he or she is often not the only player in the game. There are several others that serve particular roles in keeping the industry viable. There are recruiters who are typically responsible for initially approaching and engaging youth to be trafficked. Groomers are those who teach inducted victims the business. They may dress them or physically prepare them as well as teach them how to entertain customers effectively and efficiently. Customers must be made to believe that victims want to be there and are happy to be engaged in a sexual liaison with them. Security or "watchers" are people hired to watch victims that dance in night clubs, or they drive victims to truck stops or dates, making sure victims that go into a customer's home or motel room come out paid and unharmed.

Connectors are people that hang out in neighborhoods and are present at particular social situations and events. When they see a young person who appears to be vulnerable in some way, they offer to hook them up with a place to stay, especially if they are a runaway, offering them ways to make money if they appear to be lacking basic needs. Connectors don't formally work for traffickers, but they are familiar with certain traffickers and may get small perks for introducing them to potential victims. For instance, they may get extra drinks at the club or a few blunts or may be held in favor with a powerful trafficker, which can go a long way in the event that they find themselves in need one day. In more successful trafficking rings, these positions are held by different individuals. In a less organized and successful business, these roles may overlap or may be held by more than one person.

Women and youth under the control of a pimp are "family," and in some pimp families, women and girls are considered wife-in-laws, relegated to different tiers of importance and seniority. One woman is known as the "bottom" or "bottom bitch," akin to an assistant manager. She knows the most about the business, but doesn't know everything, because, in the pimping world, "The game is sold, but never told." Only the pimp has supreme knowledge, and the bottom knows what she needs to know to make him successful. Her job is to train the other women out on the "track" to sell sex efficiently and effectively. She may go with the other girls to some of their visits with men to watch, or if the customer wants to pay more, she may join in.

Most pimps prefer their victims to date older white men. In fact, when I interviewed women in prostitution they also admitted they preferred dating older white men. They explained that older white men were less violent, had money, and might even provide a tip. However, addiction to drugs and the stress of bringing in a nightly quota overrode who victims and women in prostitution were likely to have paid sex with.

American youth are often recruited by pimps or their recruiters or connectors in those spaces and places in communities known to be safe. Recruitment doesn't typically happen in seedy bus stations where pimps are meeting runaways, or in back allies where kids are lured, as portrayed in films and on television. Recruitment occurs right out in the open, in seemingly safe places. These are places where parents believe their children are safe. These places include friend's and family's houses, malls, teen hangout spots, at the corner store, on the bus, and at parties, to name a few. Vulnerable youth may meet a trafficker or recruiter while they are sitting in the juvenile justice center, waiting to be called back to see their probation officer, or they may be recruited while ordered to engage in a social service group. Why? Because they are places where vulnerable kids are, and often, recruiters are simply other teens, sent out by their pimp.

The trafficker or recruiter isn't typically a scary, creepy guy, approaching young people. In Ohio, like many places, it's more common for a female to make the initial approach. This female may be of similar age to the intended victim. They approach the young person in order to befriend them, eventually introducing them to the trafficker, as it was in my case with Dana and Jessie. The recruiter may be an adult woman that presents herself as a mother figure, or the type of cool adult woman that almost every teen wants to hang out with. The recruiter may be a teen boy that approaches a young girl, telling her that she is beautiful, doting on her until he can introduce her to the trafficker. It will all appear very innocent, as it is intended. Youth are often approached by safe looking people in safe looking spaces. We have a saying in our work: "Open spaces, secret places." That's why trafficking is so successful. The recruiter and the trafficker will attempt to fill any emotional, physical, or psychological void and become that thing a vulnerable youth needs.

Online, a young person may be approached using the same techniques. The intended target is innocently scrolling, posting pictures and feelings, or hoping to chat with interesting people when they are approached. Using the same principles as in the real world, the trafficker is hoping to enter the young person's life and fill a void. Young people have wishes, wants, and desires, and they also have problems and needs, and access to social media serves as a potential outlet for them. No matter which social media platform might be used, the needs of youth remain the same.

The need to be understood is significant in teens, and a potential victim might post something like, "Nobody gets me." A trafficker will respond by letting the young person know in many ways that he "gets her." The need to be loved and desired might receive a response like, "Girl, you look good. I can't wait to get with you," which can make a vulnerable young girl feel recognized, loved, and special. The desire for a trusted friend might be returned through a response such as, "I'm down for you. Whatever you want, I will make sure you have it." A trafficker will assure a young person that he will fulfill her every need. She need not worry or look any further. He can be a daddy to her. He can love her and she will be fulfilled.

Soon, the youth is intrigued with what the person is telling them and wants to go further, whether that means sending suggestive pictures of themselves that can be used against them later, meeting somewhere, or giving out their phone number so they can engage in texts and phone calls.

It can be as simple as Andrea's case. She accepted a friend request from someone on Facebook who then direct messaged her several times a day. After a while, Andrea met up with him and, even though she was a virgin, made the decision to have sex with him. It didn't matter much to her, though, because she thought this was going to be the man she would eventually marry. Instead of marrying him, after a three day whirlwind romance, Andrea was sold to over ten men before she had time to put her shame and fear aside long enough to call her uncles and tell them where she was. They handled the situation without police involvement and asked if Andrea could join my weekly psychosocial groups.

Sometimes the grooming of victims happens over a long period of time and sometimes it all happens in a matter of hours. While Lydia was riding the bus, a young guy started talking to her. He asked her if she smoked and if she wanted to smoke a blunt with him. She thought the guy was cute and was really flattered that he would ask her. Lydia agreed. They got off the bus, smoked, and then he told her that she owed him and would need to pay him back. At that point, he became very threatening. Lydia ended up spending the day with him, and was forced to have sex with a different man for money. Lydia then handed that money to the perpetrator she'd met on the bus. She was one of the few able to escape that same day.

At fourteen years old, Sissy reported in her weekly group that a new friend of hers introduced her to a good looking guy who seemed very nice and interested in her. He was a few years older than her, nineteen, but they built a relationship—he bought her gifts, took her to dinner, and was very romantic. He asked Sissy to go to Detroit with him, and because her family couldn't afford trips out of town, she had never been outside of Toledo. Excitedly, she agreed to go.

On the way to Detroit, the boy told Sissy how much he cared for her, and reminded her of all the things he had done for her. She tried to express how thankful she was to have found him. He told her that he had business in Detroit and that he was going to meet with someone. He needed her to be sweet and nice to the man he was going to meet. Sissy quickly agreed that she would be very nice, and even though she wasn't quite sure what his business with this man was, Sissy let him know that she wanted to help him in any way possible. The boy seemed really pleased and told her that he needed her to flirt with the guy and cozy up to him. He wanted her to make this man think that she liked him and that she was attracted to him. Sissy said that she was really uncomfortable with this, but told her new boyfriend that she would do it. Finally, he told her that if she wanted to kiss and touch his business associate, that would be okay—that she should take her body wherever it wants it to go. He told her that the man had a lot of money, and that she could use her body to make them some serious cash. With this cash, they could live a better life together.

Without any escape at this point, Sissy felt seriously uncomfortable. She let her boyfriend know that no matter who this man was or how much money he had, she wasn't going to kiss and feel on him. That was out of the question. She was a little hurt that he would want her to do that. After all, the only person she had ever had sex with before was him, and that was only because of the way she felt about him. As soon as Sissy she drew this line in the sand and told him she wasn't going to do it, her boyfriend reminded her about the clothes he'd bought her, the jewelry, the dinners, and everything he had done to show he cared for her, how he wanted to make her life easier, and that she should do this for him in exchange.

From there, he became more and more threatening. At fourteen years old, Sissy felt trapped and scared. She picked up her phone to send a text, but he took the phone before she could send it. Once he knew she was sufficiently afraid, he went back to being nice, telling her how she was built for this and about the potential money they could make. He described how, because it's her first time, he hooked her up with someone very nice—an older gentleman that would treat her right. This was Sissy's introduction to prostitution. She told herself that she would go ahead and go through with it because she had gotten herself into this mess, but afterward, she would never do it again.

Later that night, her trafficker, who was posing as her boyfriend, called her on the phone. After the third call, she picked up and told him never to call her again. He quickly apologized and told her how bad he felt. He asked her if he could take her out of town, but this time, it would be to do whatever she wanted. It was his way of paying her back for putting her in such an awkward predicament. She decided to go. She wanted things to work out between them.

This story is all too common. It's hard to fathom this situation when looking at it through our adult eyes. Some of us would have quickly realized what was happening and gotten out of the situation as soon as we could, and even those of us that might have caught on much later would have escaped as soon as we had the chance. At the very least, every one of us would not have taken a call from him that evening. Most of us would have stood firm when we said, "No," would have run away as soon as the car stopped, or perhaps would have called the police. But most of us are thinking with the mind of an adult, not the mind of a vulnerable fourteen-year-old, searching for love, acceptance, and a sense of belonging.

Sissy explained that, as the years went by, she continued to work for this pimp. When she didn't turn back up on time with the quota she was forced to make, he beat her. She accepted this treatment because she thought he cared about her and was worried when she was missing. She had never had anyone in her life who worried about where she was or who was concerned about when she might show up. She mistook this for love.

Trafficking victims comply and obey with the demands of their trafficker out of fear or love or both. If not rescued, this compliance becomes consent and cooperation. Over time, consent becomes support, and support becomes ingrained and normalized. By the time police kick in the door to rescue a victim, they are often in an emotionally neutral space, rendering them incapable of feeling grateful for having been rescued.

During recovery, it's difficult to get victims to remember the hopes and dreams they once had for their future or the vision they once had for how their life could be, particularly if the abuse is familiar to them and they never had a proper opportunity to dream. That's when recovery becomes nearly impossible. It takes consistent trust, love, and a nonjudgmental attitude to begin to make a connection and create change. Without intervention, 77% of youth victims in my community will go on into adult prostitution where they are at risk for HIV, poor mental health outcomes, chronic health conditions, drug addiction, and frequent, pervasive, and extreme violence. That's if they survive. They become the adult women we see on street and feel justified in driving by, thinking they don't deserve our help since they took themselves out on the streets to sell sex. Some will go on to perpetrate the crime they were once a victim of.

The tragic case of Diamond illustrates this point best. Diamond was a twenty-year-old girl who was trafficked at age fourteen by several pimps. By the time she was nineteen, Diamond capitulated her own cycle of abuse by trafficking a fourteen-year-old. She allowed the young girl, who was a runaway, to move in with her. Diamond listed the girl on Backpage, a website that solicits sex, and took fifty percent of the girls' earnings. She helped her victim avoid the guys that lived downstairs who wanted to first pass her around among themselves before trafficking her to others, keeping all of the money.

Diamond's mother was in prison for murder, and her father was accused of sexually abusing Diamond. She had been in foster care, from which she ran away several times. Her three sisters were involved in prostitution as well as four of her friends. Diamond was sentenced to nine years in prison for trafficking a child. If Diamond had been identified and received the services she needed when she was fourteen, her life might be headed in a different direction. But Diamond got caught in the middle. We had basic human trafficking laws passed, but little awareness in her community. She exhibited all of the signs of being a trafficked youth, but no one knew what they were seeing. Diamond had been abused, been in foster care, ran away several times, and was surrounded by adults involved in prostitution. I pleaded with the judge to sentence Diamond to a place where she could earn her GED, and perhaps a place that offers cosmetology classes, because her goal was to be a salon professional when she was released. I never saw Diamond again, but I know she's still in prison.

To professional pimps, being a pimp and pimping is the epitome of capitalism, and the women and youth they control are simply merchandise to be acquired wholesale and sold. Rapper turned actor, Ice-T, even spoke publicly about how pimping serves capitalism. In his view, and in the view of other pimps, all capitalistic pursuits are about pimping and hoing. In business, someone is always the pimp and someone is always the ho. He illustrates this point by using the music business as an example:

"When a pimp meets a girl, he puts her into a coat, bathing suit, and some pumps; makes her look good. When a label meets an artist, they give them a budget. They 'choose' them, and they say, 'I think you can make me money.' [A pimp] chooses a bitch and says, 'I think you can make me money… you seem to want to.' The average artist walks into a record label and says, 'Please pimp me… Put me out there…." So they say, 'You want to go on the track? I'll give you money. You look good. Now you get out there and you make me some money. You sell me some records. You sell me some pussy.' See, there's a parallel."

The name "Ice" is traditional in pimping. To adopt the name "Ice" in front of a name is to acknowledge that a pimp can be as cold as ice at any moment he needs to be. More recently, it can also mean that he has the ability to be "iced out" with diamonds and other jewelry. Ice-T goes on to explain how the emotional control that a pimp exerts over women mirrors the emotional control that capitalist industries exert over performers. The pimp can continue to control and use women for his gain in the same way that commercial industries manipulate and control their artists for their own monetary gain:

"When a pimp falls off into a bitch's head, he puts her into a state of suspended animation. When I knock a bitch, I can mack a bitch into a coma… It's like she has never felt love on this level. The thing of it is, I ain't falling in love, she's falling in love. Now, when the record label turns you out and says, 'Yo, we gonna make you a star, and here's the limo and here's all the advantages of being with me,' you get turned out. But the artist turns around and says, 'Yo, Warner Brothers loves me.' They don't love you, they just love the money you can make. Now a pimp never treats a ho better than the money she's bringing in, so I don't give a fuck how much they love you, when Prince walks in, you got to go, 'cause Prince makes more money. They even want you to see that they treat him a little better because they want you to work up to that level as that other ho."

Ice-T further explains that professional pimps always want their women to think that he has other opportunities to "knock other bitches," or successfully recruit them, so that she continues to work for his love and her position in the organization.

Historic trauma and oppression will drive a community's response and perspective on trafficking. Ice-T positions the issue in ways that present pimps as wise and strong and savvy. He celebrates them as almost mythical creatures that follow a code and are highly successful. In reality, pimps aren't strong and savvy. They live off the earnings of those they beat down and control. They are parasites who attach themselves and live off the blood of others. They suck the freedom from their victims and wear it like a badge of honor. They pick on the weak and the vulnerable and then act as though their conquest was a fair fight they won. Strong, wise, and savvy men find that behavior disgusting and weak, and they fight against it.

Much like I did, Ice-T lived through the seventies, and his perspective is shaped by the realities of the poor black communities in that era, when pimping was more visible. Those times are memorialized in movies, songs, and books. Blaxploitation films like *The Mack*, *Superfly*, *Willie Dynamite*, and *The Candy Tangerine Man* were popular in the black community. But *The Mack* was the most popular. I saw *The Mack* at least ten times as a teenager and I was taught to see it through the lens of men. I celebrated Max Julien, who starred as "Goldie," a pimp who manipulated and lived off of women's earnings.

Pimping was never accepted by most in poor black and brown communities, but there wasn't a public outcry against it either. And because of the discrimination and blocked opportunities the community experienced, villainous heroes who were successful in the underground market were celebrated. They are celebrated by some in the community for being able to take care of their families, provide drug dealing jobs for inner city youth, and the parade of their success in the cars they drive, the cash they carry, and the women they have. We watch these movies and are taught to root for the bad guys, forgetting they seek to enslave and destroy vulnerable girls and women. These movies about pimps glorified trafficking, and I did exactly what that society wanted me to. I looked up to these pimps while revering the women as weak and stupid, like they deserved to be taken advantage of.

Perceiving victims as weak-minded women allowed society to more easily justify the commercial exploitation of women and girls. Researchers did not and still do not take this history and perspective into consideration. Organizations often don't consider the cultural phenomenon of this history in their programming. Although youth of color are at higher risk for trafficking, no one is running to black and brown neighborhoods with a new message and a marketing strategy to change this lingering perspective. The larger society has learned about sex trafficking and their emphasis is on telling the world it exists. But without a clear understanding of who American sex trafficking disproportionately affects, we're only engaging with populations with which we are most comfortable. This often translates into the protection of middle class white children. There is a focus on conducting human trafficking 101 presentations to save children, but no one is focused on going into neighborhoods of color to deliver the message. Do all children's lives matter? It's critical that we be uncomfortable and work to educate the communities most at risk so we can change the perspective and the messages in these communities.

Today, pimping isn't as glorified. It is a caricature of what it once was. Eddie Griffith and Katt Williams have turned pimping into comedy in movies and in stand-up bits. But while Snoop Dog and Ice-T proudly announce they were once pimps, no one turns off the television or refuses to watch them because of their past victimization of women and maybe youth. Instead of serving as the butt of a joke or a badge of honor, the urban, poor black community should see what pimps have done to women and youth as appalling, not funny or celebratory. But they don't because those lingering perspectives from the sixties and seventies still exist.

In prisons, pimps are still revered. Even though child molesters are demonized in prison, traffickers who sell children are seen as successful, intelligent entrepreneurs. Until we change this perspective, there will not be outrage. Black men are going to jail and being shot by police at disproportionate rates. As a result, there is an emphasis on having a national conversation about mass incarceration and police shootings in black communities, yet the black community remains silent about the trafficking of black women and girls. We can't make signifcant progress in a conversation we aren't having. While black men are being killed and incarcerated at disproportionate rates, black women and girls are also being trafficked and killed.

The stress that black women face in the U.S. is having a significant impact on the their lives and the lives of their babies. Despite the four multi-million dollar hospital systems located in Toledo, according to the Ohio Department of Health, the state ranks among the bottom of those states with poor birth outcomes for black babies. According to the Center for Community Solutions, a black woman with a college degree has a probability of having a poorer birth outcome than a white woman with an eighth grade education. When comparing the birth rates of Africans who recently arrive to the U.S. and the birth rates of Africans over time, there is a significant rise in poor birth outcomes of Africans who have spent time in America. Researchers suggest that it is due to racism and the added stress that black women face. Yes, black women are making great strides in education and in the work place, but it is costing them their health and the health of their unborn babies. We can no longer afford to tell black women, or any woman, that she has to wait for society to think she is important enough to address her concerns and grievances on a local and national level. We are de-valuing women as early as conception, perpetuating a cycle and narrative of abuse.

The faith-based community has been shoulder-to-shoulder, fighting this battle across all faiths. Catholic nuns have taken a worldwide stance against trafficking, and I hear that's the only thing they may have unanimously agreed on without much discussion or debate. I'm frankly surprised at the level of commitment and radical indignation of nuns in fighting this battle for the rights of others. I'm impressed, and I call them the hidden feminists of our day.

The black church is the hub of many communities, and has the power to change this paradigm. However, churches located in poor urban areas are often overwhelmed with so many issues within its congregation that it's hard for them to prioritize. But churches are often the first responders in black and brown communities. Many times, they are on the scene, providing services before the rest of the world knows there is a problem. However, their perspective about women and girls may color their choices. If the pastor and congregation in these communities defines at-risk girls as "fast little girls" then they are not as likely to be as vocal in sending a message that holds adult males accountable for the sexual exploitation of teens, believing that some girls are partly culpable for their own victimization. This provides a subtle and implicit permission in these communities. Silence from churches may be translated into passive permission, but it's not so silent in my community anymore.

In 2019, three black pastors were convicted of trafficking. Although the neighborhood is currently "woke" in light of all the media coverage of these crimes, my fear, of course, is that churches in my community will once again slip into silence and allow pastors and churches to abuse thier power—to use Ice-T's words, "Be macked into a coma," serving men's agendas while maintaining the outward appearance of organized religion.

The research on prostitution doesn't address the lingering cultural biases held and perpetuated in inner cities and prisons. It doesn't address the differences between the way we consciously or subconsciously protect middle class white children more effectively than poor black and brown children. And most importantly, it doesn't acknowledge and abstain from the objectification of poor women and girls, and the cultural perception that tafficking victims are weak-minded women who choose to sell themselves for money. Society chooses to stay politically correct instead of addressing the damaging perspectives held in black and brown inner city communities. While American pimps are taking advantage of our inability to tackle these socioeconomic concerns, women and youth of color are being trafficked and killed, or don't have access to any effective programming because those programs have yet to evolve in the wake of proper and extensive research—research that is yet nonexistent.

CHAPTER TWENTY-TWO
Broken Systems

Every one says they don't want to see any children fall through the cracks. What they imply is that while there are solid, functioning agencies at work, sometimes children get lost or fall between these agencies and don't get the services they need. But the reality is that no child falls through the cracks, it's that agencies fail children because the agencies themselves—the bureaucratic systems in place—are cracked to the point that they are broken, rendering them largely incapable of effectively helping victims and enacting widespread change. We have to fix our broken systems and prepare them to be responsive.

In 2000, when the Trafficking Victims Protection Act passed, the U.S. government developed a nationwide campaign that called on professionals from various backgrounds to "Rescue and Restore" victims. Rescue is under the purview of the criminal justice system. For decades before the laws changed, police officers arrested and stigmatized kids.

They held youth more responsible than the adults that bought and sold them. Rachel Lloyd of the GEMS program has once said something like this, "Why is it that when a fourteen-year-old is sold to a thirty-year-old by a forty-year-old, that the fourteen-year-old is held most responsible?" It's a rhetorical question, but the answer may be rooted in good ol' fashion sexism.

The patriarchy deems that men shouldn't be held accountable for their sexual urges, implying that they can't help them. We expect women to respond accordingly to this by ceasing to allure men through clothing or physical assets, even when women actually have no control over the way their bodies are perceived. The psychologically oppressive nature of this hierarchy of thinking deeply affects sex workers in that even though the sex worker is only active part of time time, she is perceived to be a full time whore, while the men who patronize her services are perceived to be part time customers. His actions are not connected to his character, instead they are driven by his urges, that are brought on by her, while the sex worker's character is deemed that of a whore—a label that colors all content of her character. Norma Hotaling, a previous anti-trafficking advocate, once said in a presentation that this is evident when we call men who purchase sex from youth a "John." But he's not a "John," he is a child molester and perhaps a sexual predator in that he seeks out and engages in paid sex with children.

Since the passing of the Trafficking Victims Protection Act of 2000, we are finally standing on the right side of justice when it comes to kids. Youth are victims of this horrible crime and the law now holds traffickers accountable. But once a young person who is a victim at seventeen years and 364 days turns eighteen, she is a criminal. Much like the criminal justice mindset of the good guys and the bad guys, we are choosing to prosecute one and save the other, even though there are few distinguishing differences other than our legal definitions of who is deserving and not deserving of humane care.

Instead of a "Rescue and Restore" paradigm, we should be focused on a "Human Rights" paradigm so that we work to ensure every human being has rights and can exercise those rights as protected citizens around the world. Individuals with rights can fully participate in society by having access to participate in the economy and obtain livable wage jobs, access to good healthcare, and justice in the courts. A "Rescue and Restore" paradigm means that police will continue to rescue an endless supply of victims, fueled by an unjust society where we breed vulnerability and continue to deny full access to human rights.

Under the current paradigm, once the investigators "rescue" a victim, they often pass the victim off to the social services system. Because it's an open investigation, police task forces won't mention that a client may soon be referred for services. Holding on to this confidential stance with trusted collaborators often inhibits a social services agency's ability to properly prepare to receive new clients.

With or without proper notice, some social services systems insist on providing generalized social services to a population that is in need of highly specialized care. Some social workers want to continue to provide the type of care they have always provided and some agencies prefer clients fit in to the existing services they provide. When it doesn't work, social workers may say the client is noncompliant and unmotivated. Further, there is little regard when looking at the types of services they offer, the times they offer them, and whether or not those services are trauma-informed. Sometimes clients are right to avoid a particular agency or service in favor of not being re-traumatized. As long as social services agencies continue to be guided by intricate policies, cookie cutter options, and daytime corporate hours, they will be a mismatch to what victims need.

Housing and transportation remain a continued barrier in the social services field. I can promise you that very few social workers across cities in America understand how to access immediate, affordable, and safe housing for their clients. They assist their clients in filling out applications, they wade through the housing maze and bureaucracy associated with it, and then they wait. And because victims have been forced by their trafficker to commit other crimes, and because traffickers also steal victims' credit and open fraudulent accounts in their name, they are often locked out of safe and affordable housing.

Transportation is an ongoing battle. As long as clients cannot get to wonderful, quality services, those services will remain unavailable to the people who need them the most. Most times, transportation is not built into the system of services. Sometimes we let our moral attitudes get in the way of excellent services by saying things like, "Well, if they want the service bad enough, they'll get here," instead of saying, "Let's remove as many barriers to our services as possible by picking them up."

The mental health system believes that having a counseling session for one hour a week after a client returns to their environment is sufficient and makes a difference. But the trafficker is often engaging with his victim twenty-four hours a day, seven days a week, offering the victim a place to stay, food, travel, and love, even though it is abusive and exploitative and dangerous. Our mental health and social services systems combined may offer up to four hours a week of support, and that would be considered intensive. We are circling the wagons while our competition has nuclear capabilities, and we wonder why we aren't making much progress. A mental health system, pinned under the thumb of insurance companies, that is not involved in a collaboration or a team that works with the client will remain largely irrelevant in the client's life.

Survivor leaders fight for their rightful place in the ecosystem of helping. They come to the table as the rightful contributors to the helping process. We should honor and respect the expertise they bring, but instead, we underestimate their skills and talents while under valuing their lived experience. Their unique skillset is one that brings authenticity, trustworthiness, and experience. They are able to hold a victim's hand and lead them over the bridge to services. However, sometimes both survivors and agencies misunderstand the skills of a survivor. Survivors are not natural experts in navigating social services systems, appealing in court, assessing mental health conditions, and treating substance abuse issues. With the proper training, survivors may lead in these areas, but they should collaborate with formally trained social workers and systems to bring about effective change.

Healthcare is often a window of opportunity for victims to first reach out for help or for a professional to reach out to them. There are often three systems that may interact with victims during their trafficking experience: the criminal justice system, the social services system, and the healthcare system. Victims may have had some prior experiences with the first two systems that weren't very pleasant. The healthcare system is a more perfect opportunity in that patients have typically have been socialized to listen and trust what nurses and doctors say about their care. In addition, healthcare professionals have complete authority to separate a potential trafficker from a victim by asking the trafficker to leave the room while a test is conducted. But too often, emergency rooms and clinics operate on a "don't ask, don't tell" policy. As a healthcare professional, I may have an idea that something is wrong, but I won't ask because I'm busy or I don't know what to ask or there isn't a sexual assault nurse or social worker available, or I've seen this patient beat up before and I don't believe they're going to disclose anyway. They patch up whatever brought a victim into the emergency room or clinic before sending them back into their dangerous life.

Church doctrine and organized religion can be scary to victims who are looking for a place of solace and fellowship. Victims sometimes express that their experiences seem to be the antithesis of what the church welcomes into their congregation. Victims may find the church disconnected from the battles they face in life. Some members may be overly concerned with procedure and manner of dress rather than what's in the person's heart. A recent trafficking case in Toledo in which pastors were accused and later convicted of trafficking a fourteen-year-old drew attention from the church community. A few senior pastors in the community commented that we need to focus more on the manner of dress among young girls in our community. This type of backward thinking continues to separate the church from the issues within its community.

When a victim believes that she is saved through Jesus Christ but has been shamed by society, it is in those delicate moments that church members and pastors can help those tiny wings of spirituality grow, or they can make subtle or sweeping generalizations that are unwelcoming and serve to push victims away from their church.

The child welfare system is one of the most stressed systems that we have in America. Their assessments and intervention models are most effective with infants, babies, and small children. Highly mobile populations, such as teenagers, present additional difficulties. Child welfare is woefully underfunded, and the opioid epidemic has ravaged the system. Foster homes across the country have been filled with children of parents addicted to heroin. At the same time, safe harbor laws have been passed that rightfully moved sex trafficked children from the juvenile delinquency system as the primary institution in their lives to the child welfare system. However, in most states, this has been an unfunded mandate, meaning they have all of the responsibility without any of the funding to support the work.

What we've done is stressed out a system that is already stressed. In best case scenarios, child welfare workers can triage cases, but not provide the necessary in-depth work that is needed. The results are evident. The National Center for Missing and Exploited Children reports estimate that one in seven missing teens from foster care are likely to be trafficked. There is a gaping hole in the system. Child welfare workers are feeling the effects. In Ohio, the number one reason child welfare workers quit their job is because of stress and vicarious trauma. During 2016 and 2017 alone, 53% of workers showed signs of PTSD, and one in four child welfare workers in Ohio quit their jobs.

Many advocates say they want to be the person who builds the bridges clients walk across, connecting them agencies where they can get the treatment that they need. They want to offer nonjudgmental, trusting, intensive, flexible, and comprehensive services to help victims because they know victims need the services of many agencies. But what if their client is not standing at the bridge, ready to cross? What if they are under the bridge? Because stigma makes clients feel unworthy and unwelcomed, systems, too, often make victims feel unworthy and unwelcomed.

But what if, by some miracle, you convince your client that they are worthy and your client is ready, the agency is open to receive them, and you get your client from under the bridge and across it? As the helper, you need agencies to work together effectively because your client needs more than one service. But while crossing the bridge, you find out that the bridge you're walking across isn't strong, it's rickety, and a few slats in the bridge are unhealthy and weak. Perhaps some of the slats are made of strong teak wood, like well-funded agencies, but other slats are made of straw and mud, like grassroots agencies. The poles of the railing your client is supposed to hold onto don't fit into the slats. They won't work together to fit well. The nails that hold the bridge together refuse to do their part unless they are fully acknowledged and we name the bridge, "The Nail Bridge." And no one evaluates the quality of this collaboration between the slats, railing, poles, and nails, so no one knows if the bridge ever functioned effectively in its mission to carry clients safely across in the first place.

Collaboration is what builds a strong bridge. But competition and ego is responsible for preventing most successful collaborations from happening. Policy destroys the rest. A social worker's confidentiality, healthcare's HIPPA, and use of legal privilege often prevents effective collaboration. There are important reasons to protect client information, but when it hinders effective practice then collaborators should work to find ways to protect client information while still engaging in meaningful work together.

Additionally, most people say they are in anti-trafficking work for the right reasons, but if they were, they would check their ego at the door, take off the agency representative hat, use their brain to figure out how to collaborate in a manner that protects client information, and wouldn't worry as much about who gets the credit and the funding. We would evaluate what works and doesn't work and make adjustments accordingly. Instead of just doing something to check off the box or to get our billable hour, we would do the best thing. If we worked like that, we would make a significant dent in trafficking. But as the saying goes, "We have met the enemy and he is us."

Traffickers can't stand up against a united force. But we stay on that rickety bridge, trying to carry victims somewhere, but we're not sure where, how long it will take to get there, or if we're going in the right direction. I still believe in collaboration. Although, much like Ghandi, who said he also believed in Christianity, but not in Christians, I believe in collaboration, but not always in collaborators.

Without collaboration, we know that the work can't be done. We need each other and our expertise in various disciplines. We can't do it alone. We can't create silos. For the benefit of victims, we must work together to cultivate survivors from victims, and then thrivers from survivors. When we work alone, it can have disastrous consequences.

When I met Carolyn, she was a tall seventeen-year-old bi-racial girl who was stunning. She had wavy dark hair, caramel colored skin, and dark eyes. She was absolutely beautiful. I met Carolyn in juvenile detention. She was brought in and held because she was trafficked into the sex trade and the juvenile court was holding her for the day until child protective services could connect with her. When they identified a trafficked girl, they would also call me to come down to conduct an interview. Carolyn let me know that she didn't like what she was doing, and, although it was rare, she didn't want to see her trafficker again. She wanted to change her life. We talked for a long while about her life and some about mine. We talked for what seemed like hours. Carolyn, along with all of the other kids that I spoke with in detention, talked about wanting to live a normal life and to be loved by her parents, to be involved in positive activites, have braces, and be like other teens. They wanted the same things that other teens wanted. Story after story, I learned that many girls were caught up in impossible situations and tried to respond to those situations that best way they knew how.

Carolyn wanted a home and loving parents. She didn't want to have been trafficked, having sex with men she didn't know. She described putting her face in the lap of a truck driver that had been driving for several hours as the most disgusting thing she could have ever done. She despised it. At one point in our conversation, she asked me if I believed a daughter should be the jewel in the crown that her father wears. I told her that I didn't understand the reference. She explained that what she really wanted was to be special to her father. She wanted to make him proud of her and she wanted his love and attention. When I left, we promised to talk to each other when she got out. I would link her to some services, but she and I would agree to meet up and talk periodically about her progress.

Carolyn did connect with a service provider, but it was with one lone program provider who was a survivor but who was inexperienced in navigating service systems and wasn't trained in understanding mental health. The provider convinced Carolyn that she could take care of her every need and that there was no need to attend any other programs. All of the support she needed would be provided to her by this one person. As this seemed eerily similar to what traffickers do, I became extremely concerned.

Advocates know that survivors need to connect and build a strong relationship with someone that they can trust. Relationship building is the key to helping victims become successful survivors. However, at some point, survivors need to begin accessing other services for their basic needs: legal services, psychological and emotional services, and more. One purpose of good collaboration is so that various providers can bring expertise to the table to assist survivors. Everyone became concerned. Several providers reached out to Carolyn. I called on my friend, Linda, to reach out. Typically, if Linda is on the case, I can count on the connection being made, but Carolyn did as she was informed. She let everyone know that she would not be working with anyone except this one inexperienced provider.

I became panicked because after Carolyn made it clear that she didn't want anyone to contact her, and without the cooperation of her provider, we were forced to honor her wishes. Drowned in despair, Carolyn ended up killing herself within the year.

In Carolyn's case, I'd like to think that there wasn't anything that anyone could have done to stop it, but I always question if she was in the right hands at the right time. We helped her father to raise the funds for a proper funeral for Carolyn and laid her promising young body to rest. I told my daughter many times after that she is the jewel in our crown.

CHAPTER TWENTY-THREE
Goodbye, Emma

The last time I saw Emma Kay, she was thirty-three years old. I was driving down Lagrange Street in north Toledo, on my way to the store, when I saw her walking. I pulled over and, this time, jumped out of the car. Unlike our last encounter, we were so happy to see each other, and Emma Kay hugged me right in the middle of the street. It felt refreshing to hold my old friend again.

I went to her house to visit, which was off of Lagrange Street, and stayed for a few hours, catching up and travelling down memory lane, talking about all the bike rides we took together, the sleepovers, the mud pies sprinkled with sugar, and the treasured times we'd spent in our fort as children. It was good to be in her presence, to feel like kids again, and to see her smile.

Emma Kay had always been a small woman, but looking her over, she couldn't have weighed more than a hundred pounds. She said she was working on her sobriety and that things with her were good. I hoped that was true, and I hugged her really hard before I left.

A few weeks later, I got word that Emma Kay had been killed.

A customer of Emma Kay's murdered her. Emma had slipped and started smoking crack again. Before long, she ran out of money and went out on Lagrange Street to catch a date to pay for drugs and some food. Having driven around all day, looking for a suitable prostitute, Lee Jeffries pulled up alongside Emma Kay. What Jeffries didn't know, or care about, was that Emma Kay was a loved human being with memories and a childhood and people that would miss her terribly. He didn't know or care that her parents had brought her home from the hospital with dreams of her future dancing in their heads. No one who saw Emma Kay get into Jeffries' car knew or cared that she had a great personality with an infectious laugh that matched her quick wit and sense of humor; that she had hopes and dreams. No one said, "Stop, don't get in that car. Don't go." No one.

On the day Emma Kay got into Lee Jeffries' car, I was probably thinking about my college graduation. I was probably thinking about how things were looking up for me, about my own ascension and future—while my friend's future was being taking away from her. And I'd escaped my abusers, while Emma was facing her ultimate and final abuser. We were the twins. She was the white one and I was the black one.

Emma got in the car with Lee Jeffries, and he drove her to a dark and isolated parking lot. There, he stabbed her repeatedly, over twenty times, while he engaged in sex with her.

When Emma was thought to be missing, her family made flyers and posted them everywhere. They went to corner stores, posted flyers under bridges and near the water—anywhere they could think of. They were praying that the community they'd spent so many years in would help them in their time of need.

Lee Jeffries graduated from Rogers High School in 1983, barely able to read and write. He was married and attended church most Sundays. On January 26, 1993, Jeffries received a fifteen-years-to-life sentence and was incarcerated at the Allen Correctional Facility. He was deemed a sexual predator, meaning he was convicted of a sexually oriented offense and is considered likely to engage in future sexually oriented offenses. The psychologist on the case reported that he would likely repeat his offense, and that he is of maximum risk to the community.

I missed Emma Kay's funeral, but drove out of town to visit her gravesite. Emma is buried in the Palmyras Cemetery in Adrian, Michigan. Rarely is the case of a prostitute's death ever solved, but Emma's case was solved quickly because her killer didn't realize that as he beat and stabbed her and pushed her nude body out of the car, that a credit card receipt was stuck to her bloody back. It was a receipt for his mother's credit card and that led the police right to his house.

During the interrogation, they asked Lee about where he went that day, and they showed Lee two pictures, both of which were items he purchased at a local Kmart store: six storage bins wrapped in plastic, a box, and a plastic box of screws.

"Do you remember purchasing these items?" investigators asked.

"These two items on here is something I purchased." Jeffries pointed to the pictures, "This and right here, and that's all I really needed." He admitted that he went up to Kmart to shop at about seven in the evening. Jeffries said, "It had to be about seven, 'cause my wife left the house. She went to the store, to Value City, with one of her girlfriends."

"Do you remember whose car you drove?" the investigator probed.

"My mother's. That's her car, and she lets me use it every now and then."

"Do you know what happened to the receipts for these items?" the investigator continued.

"To be honest with you, no, I really don't. I have so many different receipts, it ain't no telling. It probably got thrown away or something."

When investigators confronted Jeffries with the fact that the receipt had been stuck to Emma Kay Dolberry's back, he finally admitted to the crime. He said God told him to do it. Jeffries also revealed that he had stabbed two other women involved in the sex trade. It had become a habit for him. Fortunately, they lived. Jeffries was able to plead guilty in Emma Kay's case in exchange that he would not be tried for the other two attempted murders.

The day Emma died, her family had to tell her children that their mother was gone, and up until that point, I had no idea Emma even had any children. At the time, Emma's youngest daughter, Marie, was in second grade, and was devastated by the violent and abrupt loss of her mother. Today, Marie and her older sister, Becky, both live in Tennessee with children of their own, and Emma lives on through them.

The crushing effects that Emma's life had on her family is a story I've heard all too often. The families of women and girls who have been prostituted by traffickers or drugs have been described to me over and over again. There is a constant fear and looming anxiety that keeps them holding their breath, hoping it isn't their daughter, their sister, their mother, who is found in the street. Many families resort to having their daughters arrested during the holidays so that they can find some peaceful rest for a bit. In the case of Emma's children, her mother had to take control, and at some point, could no longer allow a drug-addicted Emma to lie to her children, telling them she was going to show up, but didn't. She couldn't allow Emma in the house to steal from her, to feed her habit. Like many families, they had to let go of Emma, though it broke their hearts. It was the safest thing for her children.

But I know that Emma was trying to get her life back together, because she told me the last time I saw her—an encounter I'm so thankful to have had. At Jeffries' sentencing hearing on January 15, 1993, Judge Ruth Ann Franks had these words to say:

"It is very clear, very clear that there is a course of conduct that you were involved in that is one of violence, one of terror. And Miss Dolberry is and has been the recipient of that violence. And tragically, she did not survive that attack. And most fortunate is the fact that two other victims did survive your assault on them.

Whether a victim is a victim of high stature in the community or one who does not have that kind of blessing in their life, but is working hard to get their life back together, sometimes that's a more noble calling than people who have been given things all their life, and the pride that that person may have as they attempt to elevate themselves from problems that caused them to, to fall into a criminal element. It doesn't diminish in my eyes the fact that a life has been lost. And certainly, the court, meaning the court of law, doesn't diminish it and say that that life is worth something less, because the impact of the lost, of Miss Dolberry, on the family, is forever.

There is a connection still that your family will have with you, knowing that you're going to be fed, you're going to be given an opportunity to go on with whatever occupation, if you want to pursue it, you're going to be given that opportunity through the state institutions. And Miss Dolberry's life, that will never happen. And your children will have an opportunity to see you in the future, unlike that of the victim. And it must be a very troubling and unsettling thing, and all of us know the sentence that we impose doesn't take that kind of pain away.

It is the sentence of this court that you are committed to the Ohio Department of Rehabilitation and Correction specifically in Orient, Ohio for an indefinite term of fifteen years-to-life imprisonment."

James Colbert and David Morris from The Friendly Center

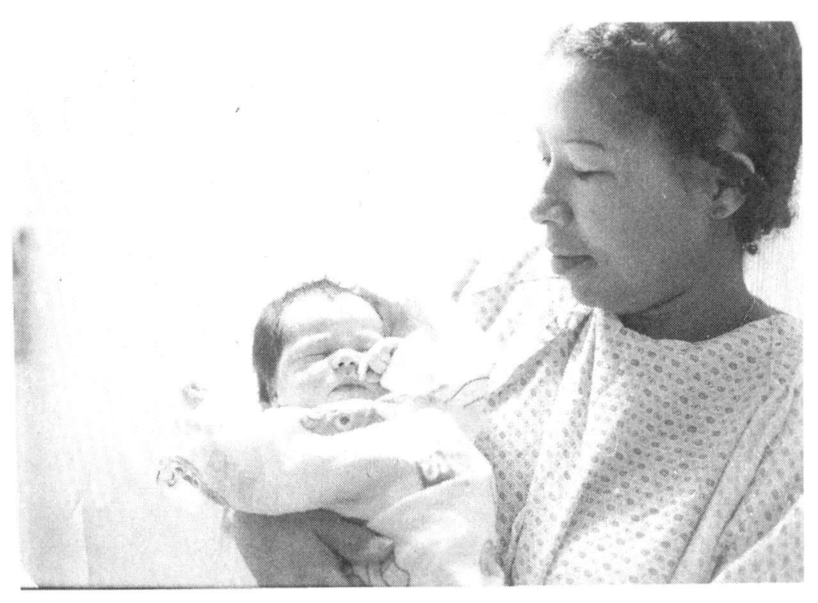

Lisa, born December 3, 1988

Street outreach in "Big Blue"

Home visit with a survivor

Lot where Emma Kay was murdered

Grave of Emma Kay Dolberry

PART III

I once heard a story about a baby in the river. This story has been told many times and in many different ways. A woman was standing near a river when she saw a baby floating nearby. She ran up to the baby and grabbed it out of the river. She wrapped it in warm blankets, fed it, loved it, and found it a home. Soon there was another baby, and another baby, and another baby. Exhausted and frustrated from taking care of the babies that had been discarded like trash, the woman told a friend she was going upstream to find out who was throwing the babies in the river and stop them. That's how I felt—like I was helping one woman at a time. And there were always more women and girls. We needed funding. We needed more help. We needed the world to understand what was happening in our community. This was the beginning of my macro level practice. I wanted to help the thousands. Laws needed to be passed, perceptions needed to change, funding needed to be abundant. But I had no idea how to do these things.

CHAPTER TWENTY-FOUR

Rules of Engagement

I didn't find out about Emma's death until I was well into my case management and group work with women on the street and moving into my work with trafficked youth. In my master's program at the time, I had to learn to write a needs assessment. Consumed with Emma's death and the plight of others, I wrote a needs assessment about the women and youth and took it down to city council. I wanted the city to do something about it since it was a city problem. I walked up to the secretary and asked to speak to a city councilman. She politely asked me if I had an appointment and then informed me that I needed an appointment to talk to someone. I tried to explain the reason for my visit when I realized I was getting nowhere without an appointment. Deflated, I made an appointment and turned to leave.

As I headed back to the elevators, I noticed the secretary get up to go to the bathroom. Once she rounded the corner, I turned back around and put my typed needs assessment on the desk of the councilman who I thought was the most sympathetic. Time was of the essence. I felt I had to do it.

Much to my delight, Councilman Ferner read the assessment and scored me a few moments on the floor of city council. I was extremely nervous. I had never faced what I considered to be the establishment to ask for what my community needed. I could do street outreach and go in crack houses, sell weed, and, in my past, threaten people, but talk to the people with the real power? That was scary. I practiced and practiced beforehand, but that just made me even more nervous, until I heard my mother's voice tell me, "Just care with courage."

I trusted in that and stepped forward with my knees rattling and my voice shaking. I told the council members what was happening to women and youth and why they should care. I used what I read in the library and I put it in financial terms for them. I told them that it costs the police force and the courts approximately $2,000 per arrest and it costs space at the jail and staffing oversight every time a woman in prostitution is arrested. I told them that a woman in prostitution is arrested an average of ten times throughout her time in prostitution. By helping women transition into treatment, we could save lives as well as the city's money.

I ended up receiving $8,000 to conduct street outreach and run groups. I stretched that money, making it last for two years, buying snacks, printing flyers, and having goodies available for those who came to group. Given my success with city council, David from The Friendly Center submitted a request to the United Methodist Women and received another $8,000 to continue my work. The Friendly Center allowed me to build an ongoing case management program for these women and youth.

Soon, I was working with the juvenile court system, getting referrals. I was receiving referrals from municipal court as well. Women would go to court and say they wanted to go to the Second Chance Program, so judges and probation officers started to make those referrals regularly.

The work I was doing was meaningful and it fit my personality well, but I started to have this itch to further my education by getting a doctoral degree. No one in my family at that point had ever pursued a PhD. My family was happy that I even got a degree at all and was working a legitimate job, because to pursue and obtain my master's was beyond anything my family could've imagined. I was no longer in an abusive relationship and I was doing well. I maintained my case load at work and facilitated my weekly groups, but my eyes were focused on achieving this new milestone.

At night, after my daughter went to bed, I read everything I could find on doctoral programs. Once I understood the system of it all and where I wanted to apply, I would get up early in the mornings to apply, request my transcripts, and work on my personal statement. I tried studying for the GRE, but the more I studied, the less confident I became, so I just took the GRE without much preparation and promptly scored a little higher than what our pet cat would have scored. I knew I had to focus on my personal statement and sell myself, because my GRE score wasn't going to sell me.

Because the PhD was a research degree, I did my homework and I challenged the admission committee to identify with overwhelming evidence that scores on the GRE cannot conclusively predict the academic success of a social work student. By that time, I had learned that rules can be bent and there were indeed pathways and roads less travelled to the next level if you had the courage to pursue them. And where there is no pathway, I learned to take up a machete and clear a path. Not only did I get accepted into a PhD program, I got accepted into two of them with a scholarship package from both.

I chose to attend Indiana University-Purdue University in Indianapolis. When the acceptance letters came, I told my family and David and James at The Friendly Center that I would be leaving. I sold my house, paid off the $35,000 I owed on it, and moved to Indianapolis with my five-year-old daughter and without any significant savings in my bank account. With his encouragement, I left my boyfriend in Toledo, not understanding at the time that Jeff was actually the person I would end up spending the next twenty-five years of my life with.

I had no idea how to live in a city without my family around me. We largely existed in a four block radius that I expanded to the entire north end when I became a social worker. I had been brave enough to save my money and buy a home across town for me and my daughter, but this wasn't moving across town, this was moving across a state. My mother was so nervous, she called me every day.

Life was hard In Indianapolis. I had to find my way around, attend my classes, study, and be a parent. Jeff drove down every other week to spend the weekend. He would make sure we were safe, had food, he cleaned the house, and would entertain my daughter by taking her to McDonald's, to play at recreation centers, and to the children's museum. I spent my time eating fast food and studying. For the entire first year of the program, I didn't have friends and I didn't watch television. Every moment I had was spent with my daughter, in class, or studying.

At the end of the first year, I met with my professors to assess my progress, and they informed me that I was the weakest student they had in the doctoral program. I was devastated. I went home and cried, vacillating between feeling homicidal to suicidal. I had been at my emotional brink all year just trying to keep up intellectually. The learning curve was high, and I had come from doing case management and what I considered meaningful work to a place where it felt like we were just engaging in intellectual masturbation. We weren't doing anything that effected real change, real outcomes.

The PhD professors in my classes would engage us in discussions about epistemology, phenomenology and quantitative statistical measurements. They used words like "lived experience," "Medicaid rich populations," and "intersectionality." These weren't words people used in real life. We read three or more books per semester in some classes and we wrote fifty page papers. I had a PhD in negotiating my way through the projects if I had to get past drug dealers to pick up at-risk kids for group, but I couldn't intelligently discuss a phenomenological study, let alone pronounce it. I was lost.

The harder I worked, the more frustrated I got. I had to ask for help, which was very difficult for me. I found one professor, Dr. Folaron, who could explain and translate things for me in terms I could understand. She was my lifeline through this process. I could tell her my fears and she would help me put them aside by explaining a concept or a process in language that was familiar to me. Though I had so much experience in the street and an urban education that gave me the knowledge and access

I needed to do my work, I hadn't been prepared for the academic world. My community didn't have access to and wasn't equipped to bring kids up in a school system that prepared them for college-level academic success. My brain just worked differently. I was just as smart, and even more intuitive and psychologically equipped than other hopeful social workers, but I wasn't an intellectual. Intellectuals would never infiltrate the streets.

Through that first year, I moved to a new state, something my family didn't do, I had to learn to use a computer, which I hadn't done before, navigate a new city, and learn what seemed like a new language in my classes. Most all of the skills I knew and used before were worthless in this setting. After class each day, I cried at home, and then I got up each morning, went to class, got overwhelmed, and did it all over again. I thought if I didn't do better that I would soon be asked to leave. But I didn't have anything to return to.

I had given up my job and my home. I'm sure I could have convinced my family to make room for me if I had to return home, but my pride wouldn't let me give up. I wanted a seat at this table so badly because I knew what it meant. It meant that I would be able to discuss the what was happening to women and children using a language, a thought process, and methods that those in power would understand, respect, and listen to. I would be elevating my own life and my daughter's opportunities. I couldn't afford to fail. I had too much to lose.

Before smart phones and the mainstream internet, students had to access readings from libraries and university catalogues. When my professor, Dr. Barton, wanted me to read an article from a journal housed at the University of Michigan that I couldn't access in time, I put my daughter in my car and we drove from Indianapolis to Ann Abor, which is a four hour drive one way, to retrieve it. I showed up to class with the article, having read it, and with it incorporated into my paper. Aware that I hadn't had time to have the article mailed to me, the professor asked me how I got the article. I told him that I drove to get it, and took the opportunity to tell him that I was serious about my PhD. I made sure he understood that I didn't know how committed the other students were, but I was one-hundred percent committed and would do what it took to succeed.

Dr. Barton was a very even toned and quiet speaker, but aloof. He was a pleasant man, but I was completely uncomfortable around him. In my mind, he was extremely bright and I wasn't, which made him intimidating to me. Every time I interacted with him, I was uncomfortable. That never subsided. I felt small. I felt ignorant. After he saw my effort, he started to help me understand the content in his class. He was known as the hardest professor in the doctoral program, and students feared him, many avoided him, but I met with him in his office when I could to discuss class topics, borrow a book, or ask his opinion. I listened to everything he said. I put into practice everything he told me to do, and I read and discussed with him everything he told me to read. In all, I only went to his office five times, but each visit was more valuable than the last.

When my classes were complete and it was time for the dissertation, I made Dr. Barton my dissertation Chair, which some students tried to counsel against. But I knew that if I passed his expectations that I would indeed be prepared by the best—that I would have mastered my craft. During my dissertation, he focused on helping me and showed up at each meeting prepared, having read my materials and with detailed questions and directions. Dr. Folaron and Dr. Barton were my yin and my yang.

Over the next year, not only did I improve, I won the first doctoral student researcher of the year award offered in the program. I had gone from the worst to the best. The spell was cast. Once the lightbulb went on, I was so enthralled with my studies that I inadvertently missed the award ceremony. When my name was announced, I was in the library reading articles for the next semester's work. Now that I understand the rules of behavior in this setting, I knew that anyone with average intelligence could get a PhD. It's no different than street work, case management, or group work, all of which requires learning and navigating social structures.

I wasn't a fragile China doll. I was a lotus flower, blooming through the mud of my roots. I was growing into the light of my future, for my family and for my community, and there wasn't a fire that could make me wilt. I would take my newly acquired knowledge and skills to do my anti-trafficking work in Toledo. I wouldn't go on to a highly prestigious university, which was the expected trajectory. My work was in Toledo. I would take these lessons back to my community and I would continue to make a difference there.

CHAPTER TWENTY-FIVE

Momentum

I successfully defended my dissertation and ran to call my mom. "Oh, that's so great!" she said, "Let me tell you what Wayne down the street said at the table today!" and she went on to tell me all of the gossip from the day. I laughed and we talked for a while until Mom said Wayne was coming back up the porch to see her again. Wayne was a stable in my neighborhood. He couldn't read or write, and so along with the many cups of coffee they shared at my mother's kitchen table, Wayne also brought his mail down every day for my mother to read to him.

I loved my old neighborhood and the colorful characters in it. I knew my mom didn't exactly understand what I had just accomplished, and that was okay. I really did want to hear about what happened at the table that day, or about what was going on in the neighborhood. It gave me a warm feeling and that kept me connected.

I completed my PhD on street prostitution and spent a few years teaching at Western Michigan University in Kalamazoo, Michigan. As soon as there was an opening at the University of Toledo, I returned to my home city. With so many new skills, I couldn't wait to get there, get out of the ivory tower of the university, and conduct research and engage with my community. While in my doctoral program, I took the opportunity to attend workshops on federal grant writing and was excited to pursue this as well.

In my interview for a position at the University of Toledo, I asked for more money than was offered. I'd learned to negotiate from a position of logic and science, not emotion. I described to the Dean what I had to offer. I discussed my knowledge, skills, passion, and access to the population I wanted to study. I had a clear vision of what I wanted to do and a plan to get there. I understood the value I brought to the table. I was offered the amount I asked for and I began my work as an academic at the University of Toledo in 2000.

I wrote and obtained my first federal grant in 2002 from the National Institutes of Health. I was the first social worker at the school to obtain a federal grant. I procured federal funding for an additional eight years from the Department of Justice to research prostitution and sex trafficking. I conducted studies. I published articles. I was on fire and excited to work in my own community, connecting university students to the world of human trafficking, and providing student support, research, and engagement with my community. There needed to be a bridge built between academia and the streets, and I was shepherding a new generation of social workers to bridge that gap.

I breathed new energy into the Second Chance program, which

was a mere shell of what it used to be. I formed an advisory board, chaired it, and successfully wrote grants to fund the programs and services needed there. By that time, we had moved the program to a social justice focused church so that we could reach women and youth all across the city. They hired a thriver to work with a social worker to conduct assessments, case management, do outreach, and run support groups.

I wanted to begin to promote more awareness in the community about sex trafficking. I planned an event at the local library about the issue of prostitution in the community, but the library board informed me that if I was to use the library that I couldn't use the word "prostitution" in the title of my talk. I reached out again and asked if the title could include the words "sex worker." The response was negative. We tried "Ladies of the night" and received a resounding *no*. We were approved to call the event "Sex in the City." The public library, the mecca of censorship resistance, censored me by using the title of my talk to evoke images of upscale, wealthy white women who wear Jimmy Choos, thereby masking the issue at hand.

I'm not sure why people came, but they did. Following the talk, we formed a roundtable and began talking about prostituion and sex trafficking in Toledo. At our first meeting, my colleague, Marta, prepared lunch for an expected twenty people. When seventy-five came through the door, she went back into the kitchen and added more water to the soup.

Even though I was a newly minted PhD with a university job, I found myself inadvertently still engaged in street work. I was leaving my sister's house one day, which was still in the poor part of town, and

I stopped at a small convenience store. I parked, got out of my car to go inside, when a woman walking by me turned and said, "Okay, let's go."

Surprised, I stopped and said, "Where are we going?"

The woman cocked her head and replied, "You all think we don't read just because we're out here on the street."

Still confused, I told the woman I wasn't sure what she was talking about. She told me that she had been out on the street, selling sex. She was drug-addicted and homeless and she read about the work I had been doing for years. The woman said she had a feeling that something was going to happen that day—either she was going to get in a car and be hurt really badly by a customer, or someone or something would show up to save her. We talked a while and I asked her where she thought she needed to go. Directly, she said, "Drug rehab." She told me she was tired and she was ready. I looked her up and down for a while, asking questions and assessing the situation, before I ended up taking her to treatment.

I loved being home because in between my classes and my research I would occasionally get a call from direct service workers and sometimes from survivors themselves. They would call when they were stuck and didn't know what to do. Sometimes they would call because someone needed furniture and I might know where to get some. So after teaching a class and because I had an SUV, I would pick up and deliver pieces of furniture to people in need. In fact, most all of my sisters and my mother have donated something to someone else in need.

One day, while delivering a couch, one survivor recognized me and asked my daughter, "Who the hell is that? Is that Dr. Williamson carrying my couch?"

To which my daughter replied, "Well, you said you needed a couch, didn't you?"

I liked that I could continue to serve in a way that directly helped the people I loved the most. I got my PhD to help the many instead of one at a time, but it was refreshing to occasionally revisit direct service work and serve.

A few months after moving back to Toledo, I was eating in a Mexican restaurant when the waitress came up to me and asked my name. She went on to give me a hug and tell me that I found her sister on the street some years ago and I helped her. She wanted me to know that her sister was doing well. This was really a sign for me that I was home and that the work I did was important. I had street credibility. Now I needed to make a difference in a way that helped trafficked women and youth everywhere.

In 2004, I was speaking with students about collaboration, about how we need to know what is happening in other cities so we can disseminate resources and knowledge to combat trafficking. We decided that we needed a conference on the issue. I announced that we would be having a national conference, to which my puzzled students looked at me and reminded me that we didn't have money, space, or the legitimacy to pull off a national conference. Moreover, they didn't see how we had any authority that could drive people to Toledo to learn about prostitution and human trafficking. I ignored them, telling them that we have to dream big.

I knew something that the students didn't. I knew that if we framed it right, there were professors who were trying to earn tenure and needed somewhere to present. I knew there were continuing education credits that social workers, nurses, lawyers and more had to have to keep their license. I knew the topic was sexy enough to initially bring people in, even if just as spectators. It was our job to educate those spectators and turn them into advocates. I asked that a student put up a website announcing our first national conference.

Much to even my surprise, the conference was a huge success. We anticipated having one room of presenters every hour for one full day, but we ended up having three rooms of presenters every hour for two days. People were hungry to network and collaborate and share their work. We had presenters come from across the country from various disciplines. We had researchers, advocates and activists, and people running programs. Aproximately three-hundred people attended. Our budget was zero dollars.

We developed conference materials using Microsoft Word, creating materials on my computer. We made copies for our attendees by asking various social workers and churches if we could make copies in their offices. I fronted the money for folders and name tags, and we borrowed laptops from students for presenters to show their Powerpoints. We had the Student Union reserve rooms in the University of Toledo for us, and my mother and sister cooked lunch for everyone.

We made up evaluations that we gave to everyone. The evaluations overwhelmingly said that people loved the conference with many commenting that we should hold it again. So, all of the begging and copying and emailing began all over again. It was exhausting. The conference wasn't yet recognized as it is today—that is as the oldest and largest academic conference on the topic in the nation.

By our third year, the news media got wind of our conference. Getting it confused as the media can sometimes do, they started running commercials the day of the conference saying, "Hookers on the campus of the University of Toledo, tune in at six." The organizing committee of students and my friends in the community were upset, knowing that the news reduced this important work down to an inappropriate soundbite. I was somewhat happy about the press because I knew that people would come out to the conference as voyeurs to see the "hookers," and it was our opportunity and responsibility to educate them about trafficking in our communities. But in addition to the community hearing the news reports, the central administration at the University of Toledo heard the news reports and they called over to the Dean of my college to ask why we were having hookers on campus, inquiring about who authorized such a conference.

Needless to say, we had some explaining to do. We explained the purpose of the conference and the important collaborations we were building. We explained that the mission of the University of Toledo is to improve the human condition and that's what we were doing by allowing knowledge to be built and advanced around this topic. Once they understood, they inquired as to why we didn't ask permission or notify anyone that we were doing this. "This is a controversial topic, and we, as the university, should have known," they said.

I let them know that human trafficking is modern day slavery and that I didn't know freedom was controversial, but I also knew that universities were built to educate and advance society by building the intellectual capacity of its faculty and students. I knew the university would allow the conference. In times such as this, universities have been challenged to move forward on controversial issues. That's why universities tenure their professors.

Tenure essentially enables a professor to teach controversial topics in order to advance knowledge and society. It enables the teacher to move the knowledge forward without fear of being fired. Of course, at that time, I hadn't yet earned tenure, so I served at the pleasure of the university. Thankfully, in the end, they were not concerned about the topic. They were most concerned about liability and told me to use an approved caterer to feed people. Having my mother cook, although culturally sensitive, would not be appropriate. I thanked them, which I had learned to do when someone is teaching and offering their guidance, even if they're chastising you. They were showing me how to operate safely. I knew I should have informed someone, and I knew my mother shouldn't cook for the university, but there are times when you choose to beg for forgiveness instead of ask for permission.

After the fourth year of the conference, word had gotten out, and many professors and a few administrators from other universities talked about the conference and how progressive the university was for having it. The University of Toledo began to take pride in the conference, and instead of us begging to reserve the rooms we needed and taking what was left over, we were finally given the rooms we needed.

In the tenth year of the conference, we began to receive press from the university. In the twelfth year, the university began paying for a part-time conference planner, and in year thirteen, the university began fundraising for the conference. Now seen as a beacon at the university, the Human Trafficking and Social Justice Conference has brought representatives from forty-two states and thirty countries with almost 2,000 attendees and ninety presenters. The ripple effect of what happens as a result of the conference is amazing. Attendees return home to build programs and pass laws. Fires are started inside the students who attend, advocates are re-inspired, and knowledge is moved forward. I was no longer helping each one. I was helping thousands.

Because of the conference, my world expanded. I've met numerous intelligent and motivated advocates from around the world who fight human trafficking. However, I'm no longer uncomfortable nor do I feel out of place. I'm off my block in north Toledo, and I feel like my block has expanded with loving, caring, and bright advocates from all over the world who are just like the people from my neighborhood. This is my tribe. They serve as my mentors and my inspiration to keep going. Because I have been involved for twenty-five years, I now often serve as a mentor for many.

Always trying to be forward thinking, I knew I had to focus on appealing to researchers. We were losing human trafficking-focused researchers to other topics. Some were leaving to focus on other noble causes such as domestic violence or sexual assault. They grew frustrated because as they were attempting to publish, journals didn't understand the value of their work. Not getting published means you can't get tenured. Someone on the tenure track at a university who doesn't eventually earn tenure eventually gets fired. Keeping researchers focused on human trafficking research meant that we had to continue to advance knowledge.

Advancing knowledge translates to better practice, which translates to better services for victims. My colleagues were on the same page.

Dr. Roe-Sepowitz opened the Office of Sex Trafficking at Arizona State University to begin turning out research and mentoring doctoral students. Another of my colleagues, Rochelle Dalla took the reins along with Dr. Donna Sabella and collaborated with others to build the first international Journal of Human Trafficking. This would be a place for researchers to publish their work. I had the conference that provided a place for researchers to present and for practitioners to receive the latest information. Together, my colleagues formed the Global Association of Human Trafficking Scholars to work together to move the knowledge base forward and give researchers a formal organization and collaborative space in which to share knowledge and grow.

CHAPTER TWENTY-SIX

Justice Warrior

In 2005, I was asked to participate in a national talk about child sex trafficking in the U.S. I informed the convener of the meeting that I needed to bring three other people with me, though I was told that there were only seventy-five people being invited. Again, I explained to her that it was critcal that I bring three additional people with me, but she insisted that it would not be appropriate. I thanked her and then showed up to the meeting with three additional people. This might be hard to believe, but I'm not a person who likes to ignore the rules. I'm quite the opposite in most instances. Ignoring the rules causes me a great deal of emotional and psychological stress because I was raised by a father who thought it was important to follow rules and provide proper respect. I battled with myself for a long time before making the decision to ignore this directive. In this case, I felt it was important. I had never been invited to a federal table to say anything, and because they offered me this chance, I took it very seriously.

This was an important table. Not only did I need a seat at this table, I needed three additional seats. We needed to speak up for the women and children who will never be at this table. This was a time when I knew kids in my community were missing and I knew they were being called "runaways." I knew my community was just waiting for them to run back, as if they had the freedom to do so. I didn't know what the federal government could do, but I knew this was our opportunity to tell them what was happening and to plead for help.

I couldn't do it alone. I needed three colleagues to learn whatever we could learn and ask for the help we needed. Once we got into the room, we learned a lot about child sex trafficking, and when the microphone opened up and it was the audience's turn to speak, we told the story of our community. When it was time to network, we spent time working the room to find out what was possible. We all told the story of Toledo and the child sex trafficking happening there. I took it upon myself to talk to each presenter of the event, telling them about the problems and the work being done in Toledo. We found out that an FBI analyst was in the room, and that she had been analyzing the patterns of sex trafficking in the country. She acknowledged to me that Toledo was on their radar, and that she had read some of my reports and articles.

When those twenty Toledo girls were found working at a truck stop in Harrisburg in December of 2005, the story didn't break until a year later, and that's when the U.S. government dispatched an FBI task force to Toledo. At that time, only seventeen such task forces had been dispatched in the U.S. They were called "Innocence Lost," and their mission was to work with local law enforcement and investigate child sex trafficking. Because of the numerous cases they've been able to break, the task force has earned its right to be here each year since.

In 2007, we started the Lucas County Human Trafficking Coalition. The coalition was born from the simple idea that slavery should be abolished. Today, we have eighty members and thirty-eight agencies. Approximately fifty members regularly attend monthly meetings. The FBI task force members are an active part of our coalition as they attend meetings regularly, too.

If we truly want all children's lives to matter then we have to change cultural perceptions about class and race. Being involved in anti-trafficking work isn't easy because it isn't just about saving each victim. It's about breaking the bonds of systemic oppression. Our beliefs about oppressed populations guide our responses to their needs, and capitalism and patriarchy have built structures that marginalized people can't access, let alone climb. To help the most oppressed, the most in need, the women and youth of color cycled into sex trafficking, we need to change our values and our belief systems as a society. We have to create a domestic community that harbors love for all of its residents and fosters respect for a nurturing environment for all children. We can't help the many until our culture values those made to be invisible.

Anti-trafficking advocates have worked with politicians to pass anti-trafficking laws, and in Ohio, this was an incredible feat championed by Representative Teresa Fedor. If ever there was a woman I admire, it would be her. I try and be in her presence when I can. I try to be in the presence of powerful women and men doing the right thing as much as I can. I try to use my time to be in the presence of compassionate people with money, power, and influence, because they have the opportunity to open doors and change the world for people they will likely never meet.

During one of my research adventures, I set out to interview women in jail to find out more about their experiences as victims of sex trafficking. I conducted in-depth interviews that took a few hours each and surveyed them. I asked about interactions with customers and with the police. Much to my surprise, over forty percent of the women I surveyed talked about sex with police officers. Some reported they had sex with officers in exchange for not being arrested. Some said they would have sex and then be arrested anyway. Some said they got paid, while others didn't. Some women talked about having sex with officers and then being asked to act like an informant by purchasing dope at the trap house or from a dope boy. The threat of the dope boy finding out that a woman was an informant was often too threatening and the woman would opt to be arrested instead.

Quite frankly, I was shocked by the percentage. Since that time, I've done studies across cities only to find that the average customer of both women in prostitution and sex trafficking victims are men with working class and middle class jobs. They are police officers, lawyers, city workers, social workers, pastors, and more. It's not the creepy guy living under the bridge, because that creepy guy doesn't have enough money to buy sex. He certainly doesn't have enough money to buy an adolescent, a transaction that comes with a higher ticket price. And at the time, I knew there were a few problems, but had no idea it was as common as the women professed. If this was true, and I had no reason to doubt these women who had shared very intimate and shameful activities about their lives with me, this would mean that there was no place in which these abused women could report their injustice. To whom do they report that the police have abused their power and taken advantage of them? To the police?

I knew the chief of police at the time, so out of respect and to avoid embarrassment, I called to let him know what I'd found out. I certainly did not want to go forward and publish such a finding without giving the chief a heads up. I even considered not publishing the finding at all, opting instead to have the chief engage internal affairs to conduct an investigation and weed out any police officers that might be engaged in this type of injustice. I reported the information to the chief and to the mayor, and I also provided them with information on how to address the problem of women in prostitution in the community.

I offered to meet with the chief and the mayor to provide any assistance they might need. Instead, what I received was a call from the central administration office at the University of Toledo to meet about the issue. One of the provosts informed me that they'd received a call from the city about my inappropriate behavior, and that they wanted me to stop what I was doing. They told me there were important matters that the city and the university had to attend to and this was not one of them.

The university checked my research to make sure all of my research questions for this study were approved by our institutional review board. They let me know that the city did not appreciate my strong arm tactics and I was to cease those activities immediately. They called my Dean and they called my Chair to let them know what I'd done. They city wanted to discredit my work, thereby discrediting me. I called on one of the county commissioners who knew me well to speak on my behalf, because I desperately needed support.

I was shaken. I was confused. I was embarrassed. I was scared. I felt as though I did something terribly wrong. The university rose up to protect themselves, and I shrank quickly, like a little girl in trouble. I wanted it all to go away and wished it had never happened. After leaving the office, I spent the next two days going over everything that I'd asked the women and re-analyzed my work. I revisited my conversation with the chief and with the mayor's office over and over again. I felt disconnected from my university and I was afraid. I wanted to take back everything I said and did, and I wished I hadn't asked those questions. I called my former school, told them I was not yet tenured, and asked if they had any jobs because I thought I might lose mine.

I talked to some of my survivor friends and some of my social work confidants. We processed everything together. I started hearing messages that I had said to them over the years being repeated back to me—messages about facing injustice and having the courage to speak truth to power, and if I considered it important that there was an abuse of power occurring then it was my responsibility to not only speak up, but to show up and stand up against it. I started thinking about what the women and youth I worked with had to face and what they had to live through and do to survive and then to thrive. It wasn't like I wouldn't be able to get another job. I had a PhD and I am marketable. It would be an inconvenience to have to move, and unpleasant to leave under such circumstances, but it wouldn't be impossible. There was an injustice happening, and I knew about it. Instead of remaining a frightened little girl,

I turned that nervous energy into anger, and then I turned that anger into action.

I called central administration and I explained my research, my perspective, and my purpose. I let them know that since the city, the police, and the mayor's office wasn't prepared to address the issue, I would call the local newspaper and give them the story and ask that it be printed on the front page of the Sunday paper. I would not be intimidated. Instead, I would go in full force. I would have a seat this this table. And if we were serving up intimidation, I would serve it hot.

My Chair, who was an activist in her own right, was upset that the university did not stand by me. She supported me as I called the local newspaper. Once I notified that newspaper and they had someone on their way to get the story, the mayor's office called to let me know that they would ensure an investigation occurred. I felt like I had experienced my own little Cuban missile crisis. My hand was on the button, ready to blow everything wide open and, at the last minute, the city agreed to do the right thing. I backed down and gave the newspaper a story about my findings minus the information about sex with police officers.

An investigation ensued. A few officers were reprimanded, not all of them and not nearly as severe as I would have liked. No one was fired. Some good police officers we worked with learned about the actions of a few and were appalled. In all, though, we taught the police department that we would stand up for vulnerable women when we needed to.

Through this experience, I learned a valuable lesson. People will try to intimidate you if they think they can tap into your fear, but I also learned to give it right back to them if needed. As the saying goes, first they ignore you, then they laugh at you, then they fight you, then you win. I'm no longer afraid of speaking truth to power and have done it several times since in Washington, DC, to the Ohio Attorney General, and to whomever else needs to hear the truth to be motivated to do the right thing. I take my seat at the table when I need to have these difficult discussions. And although I prefer these conversations to be peaceful, I will not compromise the humanity of others. And now that I'm fairly well known for my work, I will not hesitate to call a press conference or write into the pages of opinion columns or publically call out politicians, news articles, and unjust policies. Women in the nation have declared Time's Up and the #metoo movement is in full force, and I am a vocal member.

During that time, the president of the university delivered his annual State of the University Address and mentioned that the university values social justice. He discussed how research findings and our work sometimes exposed injustice and that we had to address it. I never knew if this portion of his speech was coincidentally or intentionally connected to my struggle, but after his speech, the air lifted and I became well-regarded on campus.

I spent several years at the University of Toledo writing and obtaining federal and state level research-focused grants and community-based grants for anti-trafficking organizations. I published peer reviewed articles and received early tenure, full professor status, and eventually the honor of "distinguished professor." I no longer chase publications or presentations or even grants just to be funded. I continue to work an average of fifty hours a week or more, loving what I do. I am strategic and selective about where I spend my time, and I will only focus on those projects that ultimately make a real difference in the area of human trafficking.

Advocates throughout the U.S. have worked to change the language and the conversation so that we can end the practice of calling someone a "juvenile prostitute." We talk in terms of child sex trafficking and commercial sexual exploitation of children because these terms remind us that we are talking about children who are being exploited. It reminds us that adults need to stand accountable for these crimes, not the children. In my community, we used the media to release stories about trafficking. The statistics and stories were used to increase awareness and control the narrative by teaching people how to think about the issue. We marketed the issue by teaching our local and national community about how to frame the issue. We use words like "trafficking" and "exploitation" and then connected these terms to the deeper values of freedom and anti-slavery. We trained coalition members to conduct human trafficking workshops. We taught people what to look for and where to report. We situated the narrative so that community members see themselves as active reporters because they care about kids and saving them.

Because of the vision of a well-respected college Dean, in 2015, we opened the Human Trafficking and Social Justice Institute at the University of Toledo. There, we focus on developing evidence-based models that move victims to survivors and survivors to thrivers. We demonstrate that not all victims are the same and they don't all need the same types of services. Not only that, but victims will need different services as survivors, and survivors will need different services to become thrivers. We study the interventions provided and work to build better outcomes. For every victim involved in our project, we receive information.

Although anyone can be trafficked, it's those at high risk who are most likely to be trafficked. We know who they are. They are youth with disabilities, LBGTQ youth, youth of color, foreign youth, and youth in poverty. We know which experiences are indicators that youth may be at high risk. They are young people who have been involved with the juvenile court, who have run away from home before, who have poor mental health, who have suffered child maltreatment and may or may not have been involved with child protection, who may be or have been gang affiliated, who have educational issues, substance abuse, and may be or have been in the company of influential others that buy sex, sell sex, or sell others for sex. But when we look at all of the risk factors, the highest risk factor is being a runaway. We work on prevention and offer a prevention curriculum to these high risk youth so that we are engaged in early intervention to prevent trafficking.

CHAPTER TWENTY-SEVEN

A Seat at the Table

I love strong, mature men. I love men who contain enough self-love and confidence that they don't have to take it from the women they engage with. Stong, mature men don't need anything outside of themselves, instead they are looking to give. As a society, we expect these same traits from women—for them to be accommodating, nurturing, respectful, dutiful, loyal, the list goes on—but we need to hold men to the exact same standards, viewing both genders as valuable and responsible for emotionally intelligent actions and behaviors.

Historically, as women, we fought for our men, we fought for people of color, we fought for our children. We marched for them, we loved and nurtured them, and we told them that they deserved to be held in the highest esteem by society. It is our nature to take a backseat and make sure that everyone in the world is taken care of, except us. But when we love ourselves enough to stand up and share the power with men, wielding it when we need to, we also care for the world.

When I enter my classroom, I write two words on the board, one is "money" and one is "power." I tell social workers that money and power are good things when they are used for good things. Money and power allow you to open doors, to develop programming that works, and gaining power gets your voice heard. Funding allows the programs you design to help others to become a reality.

Some say prostitution is the oldest profession and some say it's the oldest oppression. I don't know which is true and for whom, but I do know that freedom is the first fight in the universe, the ongoing fight, and the oldest fight. My people's history is slavery and so my lineage is rooted in freedom. The fight is what brings us together and it is in the name of love and hope and justice that we come together.

In working with survivors, one thing we have to mentor them in is what love is and how to be ready to receive it from friends, family, and intimate partners. We have to re-teach survivors the value of freedom to be who they are, how to re-claim it and enjoy it. Unfortunately, some advocates are caught up in dysfunctional relationships and don't understand the gifts of love and freedom for themselves.

> *"I freed a thousand slaves and I would have freed a thousand more, if only they knew they were slaves."*

There are many advocates in the fight for the freedom for others who go home at night where they are enslaved in dysfunctional, life-sucking relationships. We can only be better, stronger warriors in this fight for freedom when we are free ourselves. Fighting for freedom for myself was my best preparation for this work.

Because of my work, I learned that I am my brother's keeper and my sister's keeper and he and she must keep me.

> *To paraphrase Dr. Martin Luther King, Jr., my freedom is intricately linked to your freedom, my justice to your justice, and my hope and opportunity to your hope and opportunity. The universe is built on this balance.*

The yin and the yang. There is no up without a down, no right without a left. The sky doesn't exist without the clouds. The sun is relative to the moon. There is the light and the dark, the ocean and the land, the black and the white, the peaks and the valleys, the feminine and the masculine. A man can't be the head of the church or the head of the family, the head of congress, or the head of a business without causing a significant imbalance and the catastrophic problems we see today. He can't lead alone. The mere suggestion of his control sets life off balance. The masculine and the feminine must be in balance. They must work together on an equal playing field in the home, in the workplace, in politics, at the pulpit, in institutions, and in the community. The ocean never says it is more powerful than the land. The up isn't better than the down. And the masculine is not better or stronger than the feminine. The white isn't better than the black.

In 2015, Sister Joan Chittister, a Benedictine nun from Erie, Pennsylvania, had this to say about what happens when men don't allow women to equally participate in all affairs, at all tables, in the world:

"I'm fundamental about this. I really believe that nothing is going to change in the world until the situation of women changes. You cannot simply dismiss half of the human race. What I mean is dismiss their agenda, dismiss their needs, dismiss their gifts, dismiss their intelligence. We are now at the place where men are running everything, which means that humanity is seen with one eye, hearing with one ear, and thinking with one half of the human brain. No wonder we're doing the things we're doing. We're bringing to the table only half the needs of the human race. And I don't mean that men are doing this purposefully, it's just that they only have half the experience. They have half the wisdom. They have half the intelligence. So they're making full decisions out of half of the resources that we should have. Who gets left behind? Who is the poorest of the poor? The women and the children. She's got one in her arms and one in her belly and she's walking across the desert and nobody is pulling up a golf cart to get her. Now how can we do that? How can we look at that and not understand that it has to change. Each of us must do something that changes the attitude of the neighborhood, and the attitude of the office, and the attitude of the boardroom, and the attitude of the bank. Do something."

This is the best time to start taking our seats at the table as women, and for men to offer their seats up to us. As women, we need to stop worrying so much about losing weight and stop waiting. Stop sitting in the shadows, waiting to be noticed, waiting for the world to give you what you deserve. Go out and take it. Join those men at the table who want you there, and sit next to the ones who resent you there. You won't break. You'll grow strong and you'll take your rightful place as a warrior.

I love being a queen among queens. I am saddened when I see a queen set her crown on the ground to make others feel comfortable, or when she takes a backseat and dims her light to make others feel good.

You have to lose your *wait* to fulfill your humanity and bring your children, both boys and girls, into an awakening that instills in them that both men and women are equally important in every way. Losing the wait took me to the streets, into the jails and juvenile detention centers, to understand the problem. Losing wait helped me build an international conference and helped me build a coalition and an institute, and helped me stand against oppression when it was necessary.

And be suspicious of any religious, political, business, economy, or practice that lifts men up with the promise that men will take care of women and children. The entire universe was built on balance. Men promising to take care of women and children hasn't worked. Women need to speak up, show up, and stand up for every right they deserve.

Women also need to take care of the men who need nurtured and loved and shown humanity. That can't happen if he is seen as the strongest and as in charge of the care of others. He needs love and assurance and kindness and support. Both women and men are role models for children, teaching children how to treat each other.

Like many people of color, I was born a suspect. Like many women, some men thought I was born to please them, and when I gave them my body and my love, they tried to take my self-esteem. Where they were hurting, they tried to use me to heal it. Like many poor youth, society tried to steal my value away and then tell me that I had none.

I have been a victim, a survivor, and a thriver in my own right.

I received repeated messages in my home, in schools, on television, and in the paper that I deserved less, should expect less, and should be satisfied with less; that it was okay to sit back and let other people like me be treated the same way or worse because "that's how life works."

Women and people of color have spent generations being told that they're not worthy of society's respect or acknowledgement, making us work twice as hard for just as much. My father didn't get much respect from society, even though he worked hard, followed the rules, and tried to raise his family to be honorable, so he demanded power and ultimate authority at home. He would be respected in his home, if nowhere else. Unfortunately, it was at our psychological and emotional expense. High school was the place where I really first learned about my value as a poor black girl. They checked off my name and collected a state and federal check, but no one cared that I was ill prepared for my future. They labeled me, stuck me in the H.E.R.O. club, and left it up to me to fail. I was denied the opportunities my mother and father were denied, and their mother and father before them. I complied with expectations and got on the path of failure, choosing to reject a system that first rejected me.

In the north end, the jobs open to me were those in the underground economy. I was angry at a society that didn't see my potential. I knew I was smart, but as I got older, I began to agree with the implied narrative that I wasn't. I became angry about things I couldn't define and didn't understand enough to see it culminating into pulling a gun out and holding it to my friend's head, so I know how easy it is for young people to lash out in anger. I know what it's like to not even fully understand that anger or where it comes from or why you have it. Like many young men in our communities, I tried drug dealing and, thank God, failed. But on the surface, I could see that being a drug dealer was a more powerful and respected choice in the underground economy.

My parents tried to raise strong and confident children. Their harsh parenting style was designed to produce five strong daughters, equipped to survive and thrive in a harsh environment. They raised four strong daughters and then me. I was headed down the wrong path, drinking, experimenting with various drugs, and a victim of domestic violence when my mother decided she would become one of my best friends, keeping a close and watchful eye on me, while my father decided to pay for my college. Instead of using their traditionally harsh style to try and change me, they knew they'd contributed to the brokeness of one of their five children and circled back to fix it. I'm so thankful they did. Once I grabbed hold of a good education, I found my place. I could marry my passion for helping others with an education and become a social worker. My superpower would be that I have the deep rooted ability to empathize.

I was a victim of my environment, but with the support of my family and James and David, I became a survivor social worker, helping others in my community. Survivor social workers are unique in that they have survived experiences and have come back stronger. Instead of post-traumatic stress, they experience post-traumatic growth, and they use this experience along with their education to be dynamic in the field. Because other people I respected and admired believed in me, I went back to school and coupled my growth with an education that legitimized me. That's often all someone needs, is another person to see their potential. No one rises to low expectations. I began to believe in the hope that my mentors had in me, and I began to bet on my own life and my own success. I took control over my life and began to wield my power.

My life was predetermined. It was up to me to change *everything* about my thought process, my emotions, and to create opportunities for myself, but I couldn't do it alone. I needed a chance. Sometimes I needed someone to see the potential in me that I could no longer see in myself. I needed someone to believe in me just a little so that I could build the confidence to make my dreams happen. I'm grateful to my parents because I realize they are human and love me unconditionally. I'm grateful to James and David for mentoring me. I'm grateful for the many women and children who allowed me into their lives. They made my life that much richer. To the one much is given, much is expected. And so I try to pass on the gifts and privileges I was given to others.

I read that Samurai warriors were class-bound to honor, nobility, and service; disciplined in the art of war and justice, symbolizing strength and courage. Some women even served as Samurai. They were trained to use a sword and a spear to protect communities that lacked male fighters. Some also used their skills to inspire economic and social change and defend the honor of their people. The soft underbelly of my existence is still fragile and sensitive, much like a China doll. But in my work, I most resemble the Samurai. Much like the Samurai woman, I am a strong archer and swordswoman, aiming at my targets with precision. I was a victim. I was a survivor, and now I am a thriver. I've been on the front lines of the anti-trafficking fight for over twenty-five years, and I've learned to swing my sword with experienced skill. As a disciplined warrior, I understand that to win this war collaboration is needed over conflict, and the common good should prevail over evil and ego. The table I set isn't concerned with who gets credit and who gets funding. I will use whatever power and voice I have to make sure the right agency, the right people, and the right critical voices are at the table.

As social workers fighting trafficking, we are a nation of emancipators. One tribe of warriors from sea to sea, we are the largest tribe. I belong to them and they belong to me. My neighborhood has expanded to include the world. The world is my home, wider than my block, my neighborhood, and made up of my people. We are the emancipation nation, and I'm inspired that thousands of others have the courage to care about freedom, hope, and justice.

The sexual violence against poor girls is real, it's pervasive, and it is the poor girl's experience in the U.S., as well as the experience of many girls who aren't poor. I survived my childhood and adolescence by managing to thwart off attempted rapes and dodging sexual predators. I didn't get addicted and experience a lifelong battle with alcohol or drugs. I was stopped from becoming a drug dealer and made the decision not to use anger and disconnection as a reason to use my gun to hurt someone. I survived two violent relationships. I side-stepped it all and survived. I survived a neighborhood where you are either a predator or prey. And to think that someone like me, who the world said didn't matter, would go on to college and get a PhD. I have been blessed and even divinely favored because my God, my family, and my neighborhood prepared me to do something to help others. All of my experiences helped me understand and draw upon my empathy.When I retire, I will push my chair back, hang up my sword, and leave my seat for my favorite comfortable chair. When my grandkids ask what I've done to further freedom, I will tell them my story.

In my dreams, I wish I would have been able to join Martin Luther King, Jr.'s fight for civil rights. I would have been thrilled to march with Dr. King, but I would have been just as happy to lick stamps and paste them on envelopes to mail out in the name of the movement, because every movement needs a collective of followers to support the lead. You don't always have to lead, but you have to do something. We have immortalized this movement, and recognize and appreciate what this movement has done to ensure rights for oppressed populations. Our fight for the freedom of others is now. Trafficking is the social justice and human rights issue of our lifetime. Get involved in the fight. Take your seat at the table. Wherever you are coming from, whether it's wealth or poverty, no matter if you're male or female, formally educated or not, survivor, thriver, or sex worker, social worker, police officer, healthcare provider, pastor, church member, sister, brother, or parent, show up. Speak up. Stand up. Take your seat at the table.

Don't misunderstand. Taking a seat at the table doesn't mean just having conversation. It means doing the work. Sometimes, to have a seat, you have to be qualified. In these cases, become qualified. Let your passion take you back to school, to workshops and certifications, to your own recovery if necessary, or to the streets to learn. Whatever education you need, go and get it. When your grandchildren ask what you've done, you'll be able to tell them about your contribution. More importantly, your contribution will make all the difference to the people in the world who are yearning to be free but who have never had the privilege of tasting freedom.

As an advocate at the table, you have to recognize that your words are important. Your action or inaction is important. What you spend your money on is important. What you spend your time on is important. Who you spend your time with is important. What you choose to wear, not wear, the places you go, don't go, how you speak or choose not to speak are all important. Where you attend and what you ignore are important. Understanding your privilege is important.

Taking your seat at the table means you speak up for the rights of others. In occupying that chair, you have a tremendous responsibility, and part of that means not waiting too long to take action. Losing wait doesn't mean that I have to wait for funding, legitimacy, or someone's permission. Your crown is bought and paid for. Put it on your head and assume your role. Because while I'm waiting for someone else to crown and legitimize me, there is someone that is being subjected to slavery, abuse, and disrespect. Every time someone is beaten down, trafficked, raped, robbed, and offered nothing but invisibility, injustice, and despair, we lose another battle to modern slavery.

Every time we stigmatize someone, other them, and make them feel excluded in our laws, our policies, our organizations, our churches and other faith-based organizations, and in our daily interactions, it's no different than lashing a whip across the back of a slave. It's the whip of privilege. When we don't stand up against trafficking and oppression, even when it's scary to do so, we empower the modern enslavement of women and youth.

I can choose to use my privilege for good or for evil. There is no in-between. If you claim ignorance, you are using your privilege for personal gain, even if that gain is ignorance in the face of the darkest truths. If you treat everyone the same, you are denying their oppression. We have to give names to abuse and oppression—we have to address the oppressive hierarchies and constructs that create frameworks in which traffickers can operate. A society that favors white men over all else, a racist class system that doles out opportunity based on skin color and gender, creates psychological and physical space for traffickers to safely set up shop. Their crimes play on the values ingrained in us, even as women and people of color. It isn't enough to just fight human trafficking itself. We must fight the systems at large that enable sex trafficking. We have to find the courage to care.

ABOUT THE AUTHOR

Dr. Celia Williamson

After experiencing the trafficking of three friends and learning about the abuses suffered by other victims of human trafficking, Celia Williamson devoted the last twenty-five years of her life to learning, researching, and developing responses to sex trafficking. Dr. Williamson is the longest standing and most well-known face of the anti-trafficking movement. There are few in this field of practice that have not heard her name or read her research and/or used her reports. To date, no one has written a book about their efforts from poverty to prominence, who has hands-on experience in directly working with victims, building a successful anti-trafficking coalition, to working with politicians to pass state and federal laws, conducting research with victims and with traffickers in the name of combatting human trafficking in a real and raw way.

Dr. Celia Williamson grew up on the north side of Toledo, Ohio, a neighborhood comprised of poor and at-risk African-Americans, Mexican-Americans, and Appalachian whites. Touted as the highest crime area in the city, the north side proved to be a place where vulnerable women and youth were. Celia grew up against all odds, and survived a traumatic childhood and adolescence of her own, all while watching three of her friends succumb to exploitation and be trafficked into the sex trade. Living with the murder of one of her friends, the persistent drug addiction of another, and the escape of a third, Celia went forward to form one of the most successful anti-trafficking movements in the country.

While navigating the treacherous waters of the ever-present risk for exploitation and victimization, she worked hard to receive her BA in Social Work from the University of Toledo and her Master's in Social Work from Case Western Reserve University. During her time as an intern, Dr. Williamson learned about sex trafficking in her community and among her childhood friends. Celia opened the first program in Ohio in 1993 that continues to work with women involved in prostitution and sex trafficking. In 2009, this program was recognized with a national FBI award for service to victims. After receiving her PhD from Indiana University, Dr. Williamson returned to Toledo to finish her work on behalf of victims.

Since receiving her degrees, Dr. Williamson has published twenty-six research publications and edited two books on prostitution and sex trafficking around the world. She has conducted over three-hundred presentations on the topic and has delivered fifteen keynote addresses at various conferences across the country.

Dr. Williamson started her work in 1993 before the word "human trafficking" caught on in any significant way. However, after the passing of the federal Trafficking Victims Protection Act, a tipping point has gradually occurred, and thousands are now interested in the topic. For example, on August 26, 2017, Google word-tracker reported that, on a monthly average, 60,500 people in the U.S. searched the words "human trafficking."

Wherever Dr. Williamson speaks, the auditorium is full. Her annual human trafficking class that she teaches at the university fills within three weeks of being open. She is a highly sought-after speaker. Her Human Trafficking and Social Justice Conference is the largest academic conference in the nation. While other conferences struggle to obtain over one-hundred people, Dr. Williamson's conferences average 1,500 attendees and she receives over 140 abstracts from around the world to present.

As a result of the conference, Dr. Williamson founded the Global Association of Human Trafficking Scholars. This Association is the first of its kind with the purpose of growing new scholars and collaborates across countries to move the human trafficking knowledge base forward.

Because of her work in this area, Celia was awarded federal research grants from the Department of Justice and National Institutes of Health from 2002-2012. Dr. Williamson chairs the Ohio Attorney General's Human Trafficking Commission's Research and Analysis Committee and consults with the Ohio Governor's Human Trafficking Task Force. Dr. Williamson has also consulted with Wisconsin and Minnesota to assist them in providing programs and services to victims there.

As an activist and community organizer, Dr. Williamson developed the Lucas County Human Trafficking Coalition in 2009. This sixty-five-member, thirty-eight-agency coalition remains active in Lucas County, educating about 6,000 people each year and working with the FBI, child protection services, juvenile court, and others to restore the lives of victims. The coalition has effectively worked with Ohio legislators to successfully pass three state anti-trafficking laws and, with the support of Ohio Senator Sherrod Brown and Senator Rob Portman, critical federal laws.

Since 2014, Dr. Williamson has served as the Director of the Human Trafficking and Social Justice Institute and Chair of the School of Social Justice at the University of Toledo.

Made in the USA
Lexington, KY
30 October 2019